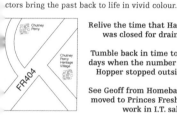

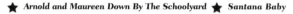

PENGUIN BOOKS

Published by the Penguin Group
Penguin Books Ltd, 80 Strand, London WC2R 0RL, England
Penguin Group (USA), Inc., 375 Hudson Street, New York, New York 10014, USA
Penguin Books Australia Ltd, 250 Camberwell Road,
Camberwell, Victoria 3124, Australia
Penguin Books Canada Ltd, 10 Alcorn Avenue, Toronto, Ontario, Canada M4V 3B2
Penguin Books India (P) Ltd, 11 Community Centre,
Panchsheel Park, New Delhi – 110 017, India
Penguin Books (NZ) Ltd, Cnr Rosedale and Airborne Roads,
Albany, Auckland, New Zealand
Penguin Books (South Africa) (Pty) Ltd, 24 Sturdee Avenue,
Rosebank 2196, South Africa

Penguin Books Ltd, Registered Offices: 80 Strand, London WC2R 0RL, England

www.penguin.com

Published in Penguin Books 2003
1

Created, written, illustrated and designed by The Framley Examiner
with apologies to everyone who has ever designed anything.

All illustrations are by the authors or from their private collections,
otherwise supplied by Clipart.com with the exception of the following:
Alfred Hitchcock and David Hasselhoff photographs courtesy of Corbis;
World's Fair pictures courtesy of the Prelinger Archive;
Jamie's Loft photograph courtesy of Istockphoto.com.
Photographs of statues and models taken at Blackgang Chine, Isle of Wight.

Printed in Great Britain by Butler and Tanner Ltd, Frome, Somerset

Thanks to Rowland White, Cat Ledger,
John Peel, Billy Bragg and Prof. Stephen Hawking

www.framleyexaminer.com

In memory of John Dykes, 1971 - 2003
"If you see a mad professor in a minibus, just smile."

HISTORIC FRAMLEY

in association with

The Framley Examiner and The Framley Museum

Framley Museum Map

This handy map shows all the galleries in the museum and how they are linked. Use it to find your way around when you visit!

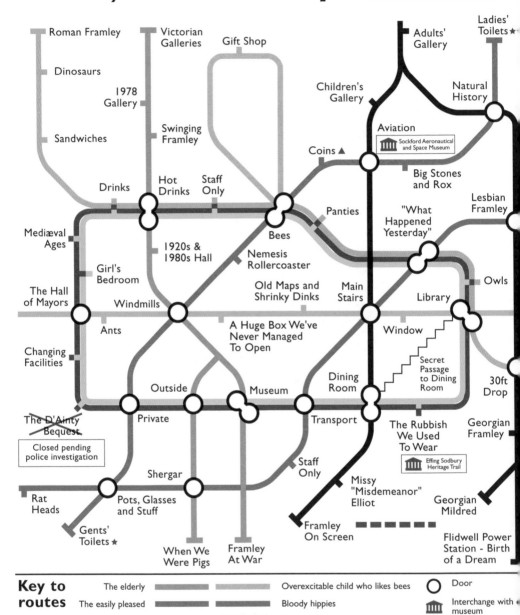

Roman Framley

Victorian Galleries

Gift Shop

Adults' Gallery

Ladies' Toilets ★

Dinosaurs

Children's Gallery

Natural History

1978 Gallery

Swinging Framley

Aviation

Sockford Aeronautical and Space Museum

Sandwiches

Coins ▲

Big Stones and Rox

Lesbian Framley

Drinks

Hot Drinks

Staff Only

Panties

"What Happened Yesterday"

Mediæval Ages

Bees

Girl's Bedroom

1920s & 1980s Hall

Nemesis Rollercoaster

Owls

The Hall of Mayors

Windmills

Old Maps and Shrinky Dinks

Main Stairs

Library

Ants

A Huge Box We've Never Managed To Open

Window

Changing Facilities

Secret Passage to Dining Room

30ft Drop

Outside

Museum

Dining Room

Transport

The Rubbish We Used To Wear

Georgian Framley

~~The D'Ainty Bequest~~

Closed pending police investigation

Private

Effing Sodbury Heritage Trail

Shergar

Staff Only

Missy "Misdemeanor" Elliot

Rat Heads

Pots, Glasses and Stuff

Georgian Mildred

Gents' Toilets ★

Framley On Screen

When We Were Pigs

Framley At War

Flidwell Power Station - Birth of a Dream

Key to routes

the coloured lines indicate recommended routes for the following

The elderly	
The easily pleased	
Dutchmen	
Wednesdays	
Melancholy	
Overexcitable child who likes bees	
Bloody hippies	
Drunks	
Schedule D	
Proposed extension to Wednesday	

○ Door

🏛 Interchange with museum

★ Closed Sundays

★★ Closed Sat / Sun

▲ Not very good

Introduction

By Museum Curator
Daniel D. Dann

If you're any older than one, you'll probably have lived through some history. Growing up is the worst thing that can happen to a human being, and it's even worse for children. I always like to think you can help preserve their minds forever with a trip to Framley Museum.

I was delighted when I left home at 28 and didn't have to wear bonnets any more. Childhood is a wonderful place. Ever since I won a Blue Peter badge for my Museum of Badges, I have wanted to educate and inform. But childhood can be a terrible time.

The Museum collects all our memories, reminding us of those things we recall fondly as well as those we have deliberately forgotten. The toy gallery is a particular favourite of mine. Whenever I walk amongst the dolls and bears, I think back to that November the fifth when my father marked my passage into manhood by using all my soft toys to stuff a Guy.

The first word I ever said was "Museum" and the second was "Museums". And this was two years before I could talk. I have no recollection of my childhood and that is probably a good thing because it was wonderful. Which is why I feel I have the luckiest job in the world.

The museum is divided into 37 sections; "Blue", and "Orange". I am 43. Why not look round the garden?

Love

Dan.

Meet your journalists

The award-winning Framley Examiner team behind this book.

Jesus Chigley wrote the first article ever published in the Framley Examiner and spends most of his time reminding his colleagues of this fact.

Challenger Putney enjoys reporting (council-related issues. He lives in Sockfo with his wife, Sue, and the Lady Mayore and Mayor William D'Ainty.

Ursula Cloybeam is the Examiner's Arts Correspondent and is still rather too involved with secret local society The Wripple Vetivers, Ursula.

Taunton Mishap has worked in region journalism for 40 years. In 1971 his rep on the rescue of a man trapped inside beehive won an award.

Stan Rubbish has covered darts for Framley's traditional favourite since 1978 since 1979. Stan is often to be seen awake and has a tattoo of Jocky Wilson on his neck.

Adam Wrent was once on the shortlist replace Alice Beer on the BBC consum programme *Watchdog*. His failed audition h left him bitter and divorced with two so

Katie Blirdsnest studied Hard at De Montfort University where she achieved a respectable 2:2 draw. Katy's ambition is to file a piece that doesn't need subbing.

Bunco Booth's life has been blighted his unrequited love for Katie Blirdsne since he first met her in November 199€

Bowery Tarpaulin certainly makes the most of his spare time! Bowery, 29, likes nothing better than to spend his days in the company of imaginary morris dancers who wipe their

Arbroath Smokie is a charming remind of the days of yesterdays. His article favour of badger-baiting recently earn him a well-deserved 12 week suspensio

Pigshit Nelson had always wanted to write for the Examiner since he was a little girl. Following the operation he finally passed the interview for the position of Sports Editor.

Damiun Clavalier is the son of int national fridge magnate Garuth Claval and often jokes that he shouldn't have work just to justify his eventual inheritan

Pharaoh Clutchstraw, Sciencexpert, was transferred from the Glockton Advertiser for £20,000 rising to £25,000 dependent on front page appearances.

Oliver Singultus-Hiccup spends m days in whichever car he's reviewing do 102mph on the A999 somewhere betwe Sockford and Whoft. Oliver has nine poin

Arcady Belvedere smells of pickled onions and cat sick on alternate days and writes about local history that nobody else can seem to remember.

Beaky Coxwain's life has been bligh by her unrequited love for Katie Blirdsn since she first met her in July 1998.

Odgar Cushion died sometime between 1994 and 2012. His *We'll Fancy That* column is continued by his nephew, Odnald, who continues to be his nephew.

The Framley Examine
Framley's Traditional Favourite Since 1978

Foreword

By The Right Worshipful the Mayor of Framley,
the Right **William D'Ainty**,
Mayor of Framley, AA.

FRAMLEY MUSEUM
Learning from the past, Planning for the present
East Parkfields, Framley, FM1 8RD 01999 391 054

21st July, 2003

Your Worship,

On behalf of the staff and board of the Framley Museum, I would like to take this opportunity to thank you for all the support you have shown us over the years, and to extend our best wishes to you and the Lady Mayoress.

As you may be aware, the museum is planning to publish a book of local history sometime later in the year, entitled "Historic Framley" and produced in association with popular newspaper The Framley Examiner.

As a stalwart friend of the museum and a local figure of great standing, would you do us the honour of considering penning a few words to serve as a foreword to this book?

Since we are approaching our deadline, I would be grateful if you could contact me at your earliest possible convenience to confirm your involvement. Please feel free to call me at any time during office hours on the number above (extension 4661), or at other times on my mobile number (07999 725 605).

Thank you in anticipation,

Yours Respectfully,

Esther Sylvester

Esther Sylvester

Director of Publications, Framley Museum

The Sweep of History

The history of the whole planet can be clearly seen through the genuine Victorian **geological column** that stands in the Museum's prehistoric gallery.

The principle behind geological columnisation is simple. Animals and plants from every era of history are buried by floodwaters. The waters solidify over time, leaving their skeletons behind, trapped in layers of sedentary rock (from the Latin *sedimentary* meaning "sitting still"). Today, we can dig up these columns, revealing the fascinating tale of how the whale became and other stories. So why not come with us on a journey into the very first days of history!

Stan Rubbish is still the Framley Examiner's darts correspondent

From fossils trapped in the geological column, we can trace the evolution of life.

THE AGE OF BATS
present day to 10,000 years ago

women • fire • ska

THE OLDEN DAYS
10,001 years to 1.6 million years ago

bears • eeyores • giant wol

THE MMMOCENE ERA
1.6 million and 1 years to 35 million years ago

a windmill • sir paul mccartney • mermaids

THE MASSEY FERGUSON YEARS
38 million years to 67.5 million years ago

bumblebees • nightmares about dolls • hats

THE AGE OF BATS AGAIN
67.5 million and one years to 150 million yrs ago

monkeys • seven sizzling sausages • batmites

THE PRE-ZAMBIC
151 million years to 152 million years ago

acorns • monsters • clicketty clacketty crab

PROTOEROZOIC
152 million years ago to the present day

cauliflowers • volcanoes • the word of our lord jesus

In the 19th Century, Fracton fossi hunter **Glorious Manby** caused sensation when he discovered th bony foot of a monstrous beas which he named the *Ptstasau*. Public interest in the find wa such that, in 1828, after seve years of painstaking reconstructior a set of statues was erected o Bollingley Island, showing group of Ptstasaur feet basking i the sun by a water hole.

Manby invited his fellov scientists to celebrate th unveiling of the statues by dinin inside one of the concrete feet The event was such a success tha a further statue was erected o the island in 1830, depicting th scientists enjoying their mea The scientists did attempt to din inside the statue of themselve dining inside the foot, but timel police intervention ensured th freakish event never took place.

Dinosaur and Cavemen Days

Dinosaurs, who are brilliant, were born millions of years ago and died out almost straight away, leaving their caves free for humans to take over, which is how we came to be where we are today.

The Framley area's damp slate soil is idea for fossil hunting and ever since **Glorious Manby**'s discovery of the Pstststsasaur dinosaur in the 19th Century, fossil hunters have flocked to the Fracton shale eager to dig up a jurassic park or two, the lost world.

Dinosaurs

e model Ptstasaur in the museum grounds was built by the andson of Fracton fossil pioneer Glorious Manby. It is currently der 24-hour investigation by a team of Framley paleontologists.

Scientists have argued for many years about exactly why the dinosaurs became extinct. Recent discoveries on **Bollingley Island** near Fracton may hold the clue. In the undergrowth surrounding the puffin sanctuary paleontologists have uncovered a series of elaborate stone feet belonging, they believe, to a Ptstasaur.

Extrapolating from the find, scientists conclude that an entire Ptstasaur made of a similar material would have weighed over a million tons. A stone dinosaur, they theorise, would have had a great deal of difficulty chasing after prey (or reaching up to eat grass or plums from overhanging branches if it was the boring sort of dinosaur).

Should all dinosaurs turn out to have been made of stone like the Ptstasaur, it may explain their inability to adapt to changing conditions. An explanation for the cutlery, menus and top hats found inside the stone feet has yet to be proposed.

s soon as the dinosaurs had gone, the avemen came out of hiding and took ver the world.

You can have fun dressing up your wn cave-lady in a series of fun outfits sing the cut-out doll below. Use round-nded scissors to snip round the dotted nes. Assemble the doll stand to enable he figure to stand freely upright. Fold he tabs back on each costume to affix he outfits to the doll and you'll have a ashionable prehistoric woman to show ff to your friends, just like in cave days.

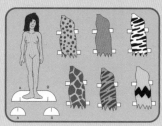

Cavemen

The stone-age family depicted in the Prehistory gallery is based on a real family who lived in Sockford in the 1940s.

Neolithic Framley

A history by renowned local archaelaeologist
Rathbone Twiddrington.

The Stones

The **Framley Stones** are one of the country's oldest things, and predate Stonehenge by absolutely ages. Though the circle still has the power to impress, comparatively little of its original grandeur remains. Several of the uprights have been worn to stumps by erosion from thousands of tourists looking at them, and many of the central stones were smashed in the eighteenth century in an attempt to make the monument spell "good morning" when viewed from a balloon.

The exact purpose of the structure is still shrouded in mystery. The processional Cursus at the SW corner would seem to indicate a ceremonial or religious function, but the discovery of an almost complete set of ornately wrought Bronze Age bingo balls inside the **altar stone** in 1983 and new evidence of a pair of rollerskates on the bottom of **Tall Meg** have thrown up many new theories.

The main circle viewed from the FR404, with the keyst "Tall Meg" to the right, and the run of menhirs to the known locally as Pan's People.

Recent investigations in the saloon bar of the Hopeless Horse by myself and my associate Mr Oswald Underclown have enabled us to recreate the full glory of the Framley Circle using bar skittles. Illustrated left is a scale reconstruction of the monument based on our findings. The model, made of accurately coloured polyurethane lumps, is now exhibited in the Neolithic gallery of Framley Museum.

The dolmen known "Dancing Dan" is said levitate and rotate thro 180 degrees every nigh a quarter to eight. Tirel research has so far fai to establish whether thi the case.

Analysis of pebbles from Fracton beach has revealed that many of the "lost" stones from Framley Circle were recycled as shingle to attract holidaymakers to the burgeoning seasides of the early 1800s. Investment by the hippies at the

International Happenings Co-Operative and years painstaking work has allowed one of the missing sto to be reassembled from all its original components true archeological jigsaw puzzle!

It should be stressed that our conclusion that the circle was used as some sort of primitive clock, will require extensive corroboration, and that our researches must not be interrupted. Contingent upon the renewal of our grant and the cancelling of our bar tab, more exciting discoveries will certainly follow.

Long Bob

The countryside around Chutney is dominated by **Long Bob**, a hill carving thought by some to date from as early 4000BC.

Although the Newby's bag hanging from the figure's outstretched arm is likely to be a more recent addition for promotional purposes, the iconic shape of the figure itself seems to date from much earlier. The purpose of the carving is unclear but neighbouring hillsides show evidence of other intriguing images - a matching female figure, one of someone in a wheelchair, and a set of Ogham runes advertising baby changing facilities - implying the area was of some importance.

Voices of Framley

Everard Cheddareth, lock-keeper, Chutney St Mary

"Long Bob? Ah, the old feller! I'll tell you about Long Bob... You know, he was there the day my grandfather was born. He was there the day I was born. But not there the rest of the time. That's the nature of Long Bob. Give us a kiss."

Birth of a Framley

Monday 17th July, AD48 was a landmark date in the history map of Framley as without it there would be no history map of Framley! This was the day on which the occupying Roman power gave birth to a healthy, bouncing baby settlement - **Frimulodonum**, or as we know it today. To celebrate, the town has held a public holiday of thanksgiving on every Monday since. The town was even declared the capital of Roman Britain for exactly 28 days sometime between AD58 - 97!

A typical Roman soldier, armed with his *Gladius* (Gladius) and *Scutum* (Scutum). Roman legionaries wiped their bottoms on sticks and were paid in vinegar.

Frimulodonum

The streets of Frimulodonum were soon teeming with people and ox, attracted to the area by the promise of affordable dentistry and minimal starvation. After a series of attacks by the aggressive **Margalai**, a marauding Celtic tribe intent on using the area's fertile land to invent tomatoes, Roman architects were called in to strengthen Frimulondonlondolum's defences.

Expecting more and bloodier battles, engineers were instructed to speedily co-ordinate the **XVI** and **XXIII** legions and seal the entire town in an enormous brick igloo in just under 3 days. So great was the fear of attack however, and so quickly was the construction hurried through, that the plans failed to include a door or even a simple chimney. The entire population of Frimulodonum suffocated within a month, including the ruling administration and the legionnaires who had been building the igloo from the inside.

An emergency capital was soon set up in Colchester, under the stewardship of Essex Governor Oius Oius, alongside his Escort Marcus Forum. Today, as a result of serious erosion, only three mile-wide sections of the 1st century curved roof remain, teetering nervously 600ft above the town centre.

The Margalai

The ferocious Margalai tribe were a real pain in the headache for the Roman forces - and the most annoying of them all was their leader, the ferocious warrior queen **Badminton.**

Roman historian Diddimanicus Tattibii describes her bearing down on her enemies in a *baceolus* ("ferocious chariot"), with wheels shaped like fifty-pence pieces.

Badminton understood psychological warfare and would prepare her troops by personally painting a ferocious-looking blue **woad moustache** on their upper lips before battle, particularly the women. The smooth-faced Framley Roman garrisons, most of whom were selected from the more expendable under-tens legions, were so frightened by the sight of the blue moustached berserkers that they often opted to wet their tunics and burst into tears rather than fight.

This thatched wall near Codge is based on an original design used by the Margalai. The tribe employed **thatching** extensively, most notably in their typical battle formation. The front row of warriors would dress up as a line of thatched cottages, while the row of troops behind peeped over the top, giving the impression that the Margalai were absolutely enormous.

Timeline of Kings

Before the coming of the Normans, and for a short, stroppy time afterwards, the region around Framley was ruled over by an ancient line of Kings. From early tribal leaders, to bold continental invaders, to people who just happened to be delivering groceries to the palace, sat down on the throne for a minute for a rest and ended up ruling for twenty years, Framley's royal past is a rich tapestry and one which we shall now unpick with the inquisitive biro of history.

King Thybald of the Primulai
(First king of Ifsex) AD 43

Roman Commander Aulus Plautus officially recognises Thybald as King of the region. Thybald receives a certificate and a badge of Plautus with real fur and moving eyes, as well as a special Roman Empire code wheel.

King Orfhard the Sickly
AD 45- 46

King Stehrheig the Disappointed
AD 46

King Orfhard the Got Better
AD 46 - 48

ROMAN OCCUPATION
AD 48 - 445

King Gary the Reticent
AD 445 - 463

Gary's was a calm, dignified reign. For 28 years, he "ruled in wisdom and kept his own counsel" until, in 463, a footman knocked the king over and discovered he was made of wood.

King Bagsie the Big One
AD 463 - 479

Ambrosius the Creamy
AD 479 - 485

King Only the Lonely
AD 485 - 501

King Dharma the Mellow
AD 501 - 516

Bad King Boris the Enormous
AD 516 - 529

26-stone Prince Boris ascended to the throne after making his father into an omelette. According to legend, while hiding from the Saxons in a cowherd's home, King Boris secretly ate all her cakes then burnt her house down to disguise the crumbs.

King Nevermind the Bollocks
AD 529 - 531

A short, unsatisfactory reign.

King Guinevere the Manly
AD 531 - 535

King Creole & The Coconut
5.35 - 6.00

Detective series. 5/6

King Spot the Different
AD 600 - 612

When Spot became mentally unstable in 611, his three sons became engaged in a dispute for the throne until he appointed a successor himself.

King Uthran the Dog-Dressed-Up
AD 612 - 631

A surprisingly good reign, considering. Signed *Magna Doodle*, prohibiting the barons from prancing past peasants' houses wearing swan hats and waving chocolate sceptres singing *ner-ner-ner-ner*.

Parsley The Lionheart
AD 631 - 649

King Potty the Untrained
AD 649 - 700

Troubled times, with schism between the early English Christian Church and Rome. To heal the rift, Potty organised the Synod of Whoft, but ruined it by turning up eleven years late and drunk, dressed as the Pope's nan.

King Morecambe the Wise
AD 700 - 714

King Olaf the Dead
AD 731 - 845

A long but rather uneventful reign, ending in a power vacuum exploited by invaders from the North.

King Bostrom the Successful
AD 714- 716

A change of royal line. King Bostrom appears suddenly and unexpectedly in contemporary sources, arriving in court in a "machine magnifick" and seizing the kingdom at gunpoint. After eighteen months of confusing rule, he announces "the successe of his experimente" and vanishes.

King Blimey the Clever
AD 716- 731

King Bob the Builder
AD 872 - 907

Constructed the churches at St Eyot's and Effing Sodbury before accidentally bricking himself into the Chancel at Ghastley St Matthew

King Tubby the Irie
AD 851 - 872

Whoppa
AD 845 - 851

Brief period of rule by Whoppa, King of the Scots, leader of the Clan McDouble and son of Cheeseburga the Swiss.

Cnunnilingus
AD 1019 - 1034

Invited to invade by Fjast, Cnunnilingus became the area's first Danish monarch. Deposed by popular uprising after he was found on Clinton beach, commanding the fish to leave the sea.

King Athelhad the Pushover
Wed 4th Feb, AD 907

King Bigger the Better
AD 907- 914

King Simply the Best
AD 914- 935

King Aelfrath the Brave
AD 911 - 935

Aelfrath's reign coincided with the coming of the Vikings. Following the bloody Battle of Urling in 932 when the Vikings burnt everyone in the area to the ground and then raped their ashes, Aelfrath declared that the Norsemen were "greate blokes whanne ye got to know them", saying that the invaders could "crashe at my place whenever them pleaseth." The guest room and billiard room at the Royal Palace at Chutney-Le-Basil were soon declared *Danelaw*, a designated zone of Viking settlement. The Vikings would remain peacefully in the palace for the next forty years in return for a small fee or *Danegeld* paid every six minutes by Aelfrath to their leader, Fjast the Furious. Parts of Framley are still officially under Danish rule, and every year the Danish government sends Wripple a goodwill gift of a Lego Christmas tree dripping with bacon.

TRAFFIC #1 | OCT 66 SEP 67

KING CNUNNILINGUS Fluce/sax died Nov 69

STEVE WINWOOD keys/voc

JIM CAPALDI drums

Dark & Middle Ages

The occupying **Roman** forces left Framley in AD406AD, attracted back home by the prospect of seeing the ashes of their relatives being weed on by angry Germans, and the town soon fell into disrepair. For two hundred years, **Saxon** and **Danish** settlers used the walled town as a bin and by AD600 Framley was full to the battlements with rubbish from neighbouring St Eyots and Hskraskelstad.

Framley vanishes from the records completely at this point, though historians now think it is unlikely that the actual town itself suddenly vanished, despite the claims of authors such as Twiddrington and Underclown in their books *"Invisible Framley"*, *"The Enchanted Town"* and *"Just Like That!"*.

Indeed, by 986 records show that a **Framley Mint** had been established, making its own coins which could be exchanged for rubbish. From this we can infer that a basic bin-economy had developed amongst the simple rubbish people of Framley, and it is from these roots that the modern town arose.

These humble beginnings didn't last long however, and by the **12th Century** the merchant town of Framley was thriving, acting as a trading post for rubbish from all over the world. The Dungmongers and the Plopwrights Guilds controlled most business in the town, working alongside organisations such as the Wripple Vetivers and the Honourable Brotherhood of Brethren to set prices and arrange the weekly market in Dumpgate.

With the foundation in 1182 **of** St Icklebrick's Priory at Bartling Delancy, and the appointment of Lord Wool, the famous "sheep mayor", this was the golden age of medieval Framley.

If you want to read more about Invisible Framley, the book of the same name is available, priced £14.99, from the musuem giftshop and all branches of Newby's.

It's a Mystery!

Medieval Framley had plenty to be proud about itself about, most notably the notable cycle of Mystery Plays performed every Easter by the townspeople in the townstreets. By the year 1240, these had become such a huge undertaking that it is estimated that of the 2500 people living in Framley, 2440 of them would have been onstage dressed as a shepherd that Easter Sunday. This was true community theatre, **Darren**, unlike the anaemic shower of shit you paraded at Chutney Community College last week.

The plays depicted all the events from Creation to the Last Judgement as accurately as possible except that the Archangel Gabriel was an apprentice bricklayer in a knitted beard. It's hard to believe that this first primitive flowering of English Drama would lead eventually to the **Complete Works of Shakespeare** as

A group of mummers give a display of traditional dances such as *bodye-popping* and *Alchymik Boogaloo* in the market square c1220

interpreted so masterfully by the Sockford Operatic and Amateur Dramatic Society, with their high quality professional rental beards from Smurville's of Chauncey Square.

The **Framley Mystery Cycle** was organised by the Mayor, who would traditionally take the role of God in the production. The order of plays in Framley followed a pattern distinct from that found elsewhere in England:

1. The Creation of the Heavens
2. The Creation of the Sun, Moon and Earth
3. The Creation of the Fish
4. The Creation of the Beasts of the Earth
5. The Creation of the Flowers and Dinosaurs
6. The Creation of Adam
7. The Creation of Eve
8. Noah, Moses, The Nativity and Crucifixion
9. The Last Judgement
10. God's Song

The set of ten twenty-minute plays would be hauled round the streets on **Pageant Wagons** stopping outside taverns to perform the full cycle and enjoy the landlord's hospitality. By midnight, approaching the last station of the pageant, God's Song could last anything up to three quarters of an hour.

Chaucer ian Framley

"Amongste theire companeye ther was a queynte;
Dulle was he and tediouse in wordes..."
Geoffrey Chaucer, The Queynte's Tale

In 1392, satirist Geoffrey Chaucer set out on a trip to Canterbury with a group of people he met in a pub. Along the way, the pilgrims told each other very long jokes, which Chaucer turned into a book. This best-selling travelogue, *The Canterbury Tales,* has become as much a part of our national heritage as bungalows and basketball.

Much of Chaucer's original manuscript, which is thought to have been written in Shepherd's Bush or installments, has been lost - and only years of painstaking reconstruction and guesswork has restored it. Several stories only exist as fragments, including the chapter where the pilgrims take a detour to Framley.

Dr Sarah Ghostbuster of Framley Community College, author of *Approaches to Approaching Medieval Literature* and *The Fort Boyard Adventure Quiz Book*, talks us through Chaucer's tale.

This section, **The Queynte's Tale,** only appears in Chaucerian apocrypha, and few of its verses survive. In the earliest fragment, we learn how the Queynte, *"A Framleye man"*, makes an instant impression on his companions:

Whan hem speketh, none shalle heede...

Chaucer tells us how the Queynte insists that, just before the Pilgrims reach Canterbury, and in order to illustrate a point he was making about crows, they all make a 170-mile detour to his birthplace to see a *"lumpe".*

The exhausted Pilgrims ride for four days to reach the lump, while the Queynte entertains them with lengthy stories of the mysterious earthwork. Along the way, he literally *"bars his page ful apalled to deed"* (bores his servant to death) and is repeatedly punched in the face by his companions, who *"roghte nat a bene"* (care not a bean) for his *"olde stories endlesse and encombred."*

When the party reaches Framley, they finally see the lump for which they have travelled so far, and it:

dulles the companeye oote, oon and alle.

Furious, the Pilgrims grab the Queynte by the legs and bury him up to his neck in the lump, vowing never to speak of the incident again, hence our only evidence of the story being in the famous *"Framley Fragment,"* (pictured here by special permission of the estate of Col. F. F. Featherlight).

And of hys soule Jhesu Crist have mercy.

The famous Framley Fragment, the only source of *The Queynte's Tale,* was found serving as an insole in a pair of brogues in 1949.

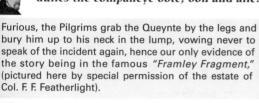

St Eyots Castle

A guided tour by DJ Shadrack, expert castle and noted historian.

"Of all the emcellent buildings in this part of the world, this has to be my favourite as it was the location for my first sexual experience. There, on my twenty-third birthday, I was manipulated to issue by the spirit of Lady Jane Grey on the West Tower staircase. Whatever people say about it, St Eyot's Castle is still the fucking nuts!"

*From **Shadrack's Ideal Picnics**, published 1957, banned 1958.*

1. North Tower Completed over 200 years after the initial construction of the castle in 1302. The hole in the wall where this tower now stands was one of many defensive faults ignored by the owner and designer of St Eyot's, ambitious social climber Sir Edward Deddewarde *(1264-1398)*. The wall of the tower is five feet three inches thick, five feet two inches thicker than the exterior walls of the rest of the castle.

2. Great Hall Chiefly used for entertaining French dignitaries. Deddewarde's dealings with the French allowed him to successfully negotiate the length of the Hundred Years War down from their original estimate of A Hundred and Forty Three.

3. Dungeon Here, the King was held without sustenance for two weeks until he relaxed his objection that Deddewarde's licence to crenellate had never actually been petitioned for.

4. Not Too Sure Bit big. Possibly gift shop or ice rink.

5. Pantry Store for food and drink, constantly maintained at a temperature of 0-5 medieval degrees Celsius.

6. Buttery In the 14thC, this was packed to the ceiling with bottles of butter, the favoured delicacy of Sir Edward and his enormous family. Historians are still uncertain about the order of these two rooms but seeing as the latter is the smaller of the two, I can't believe it's not the Buttery.

7. Kitchen Between 1375 and 1381, Sir Edward's cook refused to serve anything but plum duff in the Great Hall, much to his lord's annoyance, making this kitchen the site of some of history's greatest and bloodiest battles.

8. Well Water was drawn for the kitchen when the well was not being used as a swimming pool by kitchen staff cranked to the gills on mead.

9. The Sir Edward's Face Courtyard The vain knight's designs included an exact replica of his face visible only from the air, using two smaller turrets and an alfresco dining area with immovable seating.

10. Cook's Wall Defensive interior partition constructed by the cook to withstand the onslaught of Sir Edward's cannon-fire through the serving hatch.

11. Private Washroom Sir Edward owned the large collection of imported foxhair toothbrushes in Europe

12. Private Quarters Still private. Has remaine completely inaccessible since the 14th century.

13. Guards' Quarters Deddewarde ensured th loyalty of his men by providing them with beds s comfortable that they were constantly asleep.

14. Armoury Housed the kitchen cannon (see 1 and the clock cannon, fired vertically through th armoury ceiling to mark the passing of the hour.

15. Ladies' Washroom Still boasts its original tw way mirror, a popular sport in the Middle Ages.

16. Trophy Room Displayed the spoils of war that S Edward had reclaimed after his family lost their enti posessions in the Crusades. A tapestry denoting h father, Sir Quentin, who *"shaded pale at the sight the opposing force and thus solde his own arse Saladin"* would probably have been on show here.

17. The Chapel of St Brian The Blessed Where S Edward spent the majority of his day seekir atonement for the dreadful things he had don including building the castle in the first place. His prie eventually died of overwork during a confessional.

18. West Tower Lady Jane hzmmrvvvfffthpht.

19 & 21. Guard Towers Again, critics of St Eyo practicality as a defensive stronghold point to how th gun loops in these towers face *inwards* towards th main courtyard, rather that outwards towar attackers. However recent investigations have shov that these loops were mainly used by Sir Edward take potshots at his cook.

20. Gatehouse Due to spiralling construction cos Deddewarde was unable to afford a drawbridge made do with gaily coloured ribbons hanging down the doorway to deter potential invaders.

21. See 19 Down

22. South Tower Over 3 miles tall with one huge turr it causes the castle to topple over every 30-40 years

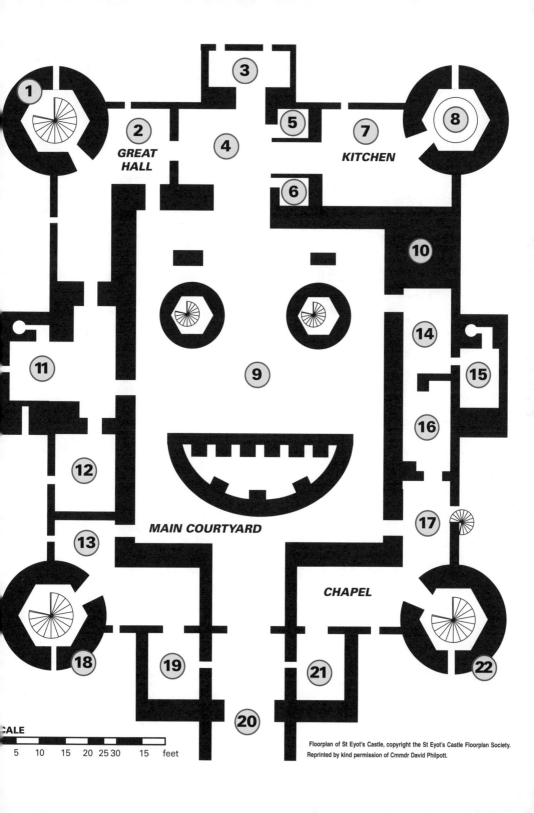

① ③ ② ④ ⑤ ⑦ ⑧ ⑥

GREAT HALL

KITCHEN

⑩ ⑪ ⑭ ⑨ ⑮ ⑯ ⑫ ⑬ ⑰

MAIN COURTYARD

CHAPEL

⑱ ⑲ ㉑ ㉒ ⑳

Floorplan of St Eyot's Castle, copyright the St Eyot's Castle Floorplan Society.
Reprinted by kind permission of Cmmdr David Philpott.

The Explorers

Framley has a great history of being discovered by explorers, so join us in a journey round the area and let's see who sticks a flag in us!

The Vikings came to Framley in 932AD, sweeping up the estuary at Clinton, raping and pillaging, and later raping and farming. We are lucky to have detailed contemporary accounts kept by one of the monks at Urling Priory. These chronicles by **The Reasonable Bod** describe how the Norsemen clashed with defending forces at Urling Bridge, killing everyone before advancing on the Priory itself.

Bod writes in a calm hand of how the invaders were actually all *"good laddes just doinge their jobbe"*, although he was keen that they *"cleane up afterwardes"*. Bod was the only monk to escape with his life when the Viking hordes gained unexpected access to the monastic retreat by an open back door next to his scriptorium. He died peacefully in his sleep at the age of 82.

The journey upwards

No-one sums up the Framley area's pioneering spirit better than **Sir Oliver Kettles** who, in 1911, failed magnificently to lead an expedition to the sky.

His expeditionary team set off from Ghastley St Matthew in January of that year, comprising six crew, forty sledges and *"more sandwiches than any one man normally sees in a lifetime"*. In the unlikely event of food running out, the team also took twelve dogs made of lard which could be used to fry up any of the 150 real dogs that accompanied the mission.

Things initially went well, with the team reaching Whoft (300 feet above sea level) in record time, but the final leg of the trip (between 300 feet and the sky) was to prove much harder. Although a **pillar** now stands on Glamping Strand marking the point where Kettles began his run up in August, the glory was not to be his. It was with crushing disappointment that Kettles looked up on October 15th and saw the Norwegian flag of arch rival Roulade Bøërg flapping tauntingly from a cloud.

The journey home was punishing and Kettles lost a lung to Jack Frost somewhere outside Sockford. He donated the other lung to Framley Museum on his return, and died of a respiratory disorder soon after, his failure marking him out as a true English hero.

Columbus in Fracton

Cumulonimbus

Framley attracts visitors from all over the world*, so it's no surprise to find out that famous explorer **Christopfer Columbus** should have paid us a visit on his travels.

In 1477, the Genoan seafarer, looking for America, swum ashore on the beach at Fracton, declaring it the New World and property of Portugal.

His conviction that he had journeyed thousands of miles is understandable given that these were the early days of speculative navigation. It would be a full decade later before Columbus thought of using boats and, as recent research has shown, it can be terribly tiring swimming to the British mainland from Lisbon.

The locals, fearful of the stranger, immediately captured Columbus and attempted to burn him as a witch. Luckily they failed because he was soaking, freeing Columbus to discover America properly in his own time and a boat.

* Swiss man, 1976. Dutch family, 1984.
Source: Framley Area Tourist Board figures, 1993.

The Framley Heretic

In the early part of the **16th Century**, the hegemony of the Catholic Church was being challenged so regularly by radical reformers that the Vatican was running a four year backlog of excommunications that eventually had to be subcontracted to Islam.

One such heretic who was eventually to suffer the wrath of Rome was Framley's self-styled upstart priest **Williard Upstart.** A follower of Lutheran protestantism, and vocal supporter of the new "Shove Ha'Penny Mass", Upstart's reformist attentions were focussed firmly on the cornerstone of Christianity, the Holy Bible itself.

is portrait of Williard Upstart hangs the saloon bar of Framley Cathedral.

Upstart was concerned that the Bible remained out of reach of the **common man**, and, in pursuit of his goal of *"a holye booke for the ploughman, the cooper, the milliner and the tarte"*, he set to learning Latin, Greek, Hebrew, English and the oboe. Sure enough, by 1535, he had his masterwork complete - the whole of the Bible set to music.

In England, this heresy would have earned him a death sentence, but Upstart was already safely in exile in Antwerp, having been hounded from his parish five years earlier by agents of **Sir Thomas More** angry that he had drawn socks on an altarpiece of the infant Christ.

Demand for his new musical bible was such however that distance was no object. Individual pages of Upstart's **masterwork** were soon being smuggled, one at a time, back to London via the usual trade routes, and by 1567, a copy of the 18,000 page book was able to be assembled in secret session in St Eyot's Catacombs, just in time to be banned.

Though he was controversial in his own time, Williard Upstart is now regarded as one of the great figures of ecclesiastical history, alongside Jonathan Luther King and the man who played the verger in *Dad's Army*.

The historic 19th Century chancel window from St Rawberry's church in Effing Sodbury commemorates Upstart's achievement and can be seen in the Museum's "Looted Churches" exhibit.

Undiscouraged, Upstart began work on his second great work - the first five books of **The Old Testament** expressed as a recipe - but, betrayed by his consultant butcher, he was captured by Vatican envoys and executed before he had even decided how much rosemary there was in Exodus.

A **musical statue** of Williard Upstart can be seen and heard to this day on the corner of Millfroth Lane and Denegate.

The Clinton Mouth

From modern day Elizabethan times right back to early 19th Centurion times, visitors to the resort of Clinton have taken time to marvel at the marvellous natural phenomenon squatting at the end of the Chine - the *Clinton Mouth*.

Discovery

In 1812, a party of George3ian textile factory workers tripping out on the seafront were deafened by a 158-decibel yawn that knocked their hats off and, legend has it, caused a nearby horse to give birth to a pair of scissors. On investigating the source of the sound, they discovered the 8ft-wide moaning depression in the ground which locals soon came to know as *That Noisy Hole* (later the **Clinton Mouth**).

Over the next decade, the **phenomenal gob** gradually settled down to make quieter, more guttural sounds, and a team of geolinguists were called in by the curious seasidespeople. The experts attempted to enter into dialogue with the Mouth, eventually surmising that it was using an ancient territorial language, dating from the time when the earth first spoke. The noise, like a clay train pulling it at a station upside-down, was described in chief rock-botherer, Samuel Hazlitt, 's notes as *"a terrible symphony"*.

Between 1823 and 1967, after several years of **coughing up rocks** and eating all of the scientists, the Mouth fell curiously silent. The team's findings, published posthumously in *The London Picture Clown*, concluded that the Mouth was *"definitely annoyed about something"* and probably also *"very hot"*.

Today

The Mouth is now the location for an annual music festival every August, when fans of rock and pop bands from all over the country come from all over the country to listen to the Mouth perform its own renditions of popular hits.

Oh I Do Like To Go Behind The Seaside

Clinton wasn't the only seaside town attracting attention in the good olden days. Although actually it was because the other seaside town that was attracting attention was attracting attention because it wasn't actually a seaside town at all, which was the wrong kind of attention to attract!!! And that seaside town, which wasn't beside the seaside or beside the sea, was the attractive attention-seeking town of Framley-on-Sea.

Landlocked Framley was granted seaside status by decree of the madness of King George the IIIrd, and attracted many visitors until 1954, when it was visited by the HM new Queen the Elizabeth the IInd. Her Majesty spent a disappointing two weeks on Framley seafront, staring crossly at the grass horizon and having her chips stolen by residents pretending to be seagulls.

Seasiders in old fashioned trousers

On her return, the Queen immediately rescinded the town's seaside status and ordered the destruction of all seagulls

Fashion through the

As the years change, so do our trousers, and [m...]
than in the world of costumes. What seems m[...]
like a real cretin the next year! That's fashion!

Thanks to the students of Framley Community C[...]

1180

The prohibitive cost of armour meant that only the richest of knights could afford to equip themselves with the latest full outfits.

However, for around £30, a more modestly budgeted crusader could set himself up with a visored helm bearing his family crest, and a pair of metal shoes.

Sir Edward Deddewarde, owner of St Eyot's Castle famously made much of his fortune from selling his armour to people who were attacking him, thus distracting his opponents at the crucial moment and netting himself a tidy side-profit.

1545

A typical Renaissance nobleman's outfit of the mid 16th Century. Note the distinctive tasselled hat.

1923

A characteristic outfit of the period, for a fashionable young man about town, of the sort found in the comic novels of P.G. Hitler. The ensemble combines classic tailoring with modern flourishes.

The tweed jacket is in Duke of Earl check, and is set off perfectly by a cummerbund, cravat and saucy garter belt in burgundy silk.

The beige flannel plus-fours keep themselves to themselves, a polite distance from the flippers and air tanks, perfect for the latest Sub-aqua dances and Scuba parties.

1966

The permissive "So Called Society" was in full swing when Mirabelle Clutch unveiled the cheeky "Midi Skirt" at Fracton Fashion Week, and it was immediately front page news!

The daring two-piece became the must-have fashion item of the summer, outselling Hot Hats two to one.

Combined with the newest mod crazes - firemen's helmets with mandalas on, shoes made out of roadsigns, or just a pair of 4" Tiny Trousers on each finger - an outfit like this would have made this grooving chick the toast of the Old Kent Road.

Local Eccentrics

Believe it or not, Framley's had more than its fair share of eccentrics and colourful characters in the past! I'm only going to talk about one of them.

Old Father Obvious

This publicity engraving from 1590 shows Old Father Obvious at work predicting some things. Note the kazoo.

In the C17th visitors came from far and wide to seek the advice of the Framley hermit, Old Father Obvious.

Obvious lived under a cave in a waterfall near St. Eyot's, and was said to have the gift of prophecy and Framley's oldest man.

Legend tells how, in his youth, Obvious had been visited by a vision of St. Barnabus the Bare who told him that, if he remained solitary and chaste in a cave for 40 years and 40 nights, he would discover the meaning of life.

For four decades, the righteous hermit lived alone and dispensed his erratic predictions to the people of Framley, whilst all the time quietly growing his beard. Soon it had reached such a grand length that it curled out of the cave and off into the distance.

Finally in 1638, two days early and desperate for the answer, Obvious left his cave. He was immediately confronted by a choir of angels. The heavenly host commanded him to walk the entire length of his record-breaking beard down the beach to the cliffs.

Obeying their command, Obvious followed his facial hair from the cave entrance, across the beach until it disappeared between a crag in the rocks. Looking up, to his horror, he discovered that the end of his beard was attached to another hermit's chin.

Obvious uttered the famous words, *"I have seen the future, and it is Bruce Springsteen"* and expired on the spot.

The Quatrains

Most of Obvious' original manuscripts are locked the Wripple Vetivers' vaults. However in 1949 th Vetivers donated a small selection of unimporta looking quatrains to Framley Museum.

Reading them today with the benefit of hindsigh they seem to predict incidents that were to occ many years after the sage's death and some eve prophesise events that haven't taken place yet.

From Sockford and olde Wofte
A mighty floode shall come forth
The boar and leopard meet upon the field
And the Bay Cittie Rollers. Shang-a-Lang!

A man will govern with the power of a king
Weary shall he be of chains of office
Much mischief and misjudgement
In the time of Daintye
And don't let him near the poorbox

Check one... Check two...
This is MC Obvious with the dope from the street
DJ Familiar, f**kin' lay down da beat
You wack MCs are all livin' in the past
This prediction's so hot you get burnt in the blast

You seem preoccupied this week with changes at wc
But don't let it get you down
It could be time for love
It will give thunder on the coast of Burgundy

A year before his death, Old Father Obvious entrusted to the Church a sealed box of his most vivid predictions. He stipulated that the box was only to be opened 300 years later in the

The remains of the box as displayed the museum. Note boot marks on sid

presence of *"Three Innocents and a Tortoise"*.

In 1974, on Blue Peter, the box was opened. Within it w a single parchment, on which was written the followin

In 1971, a hailstone will fall in Essen, Germany containing Leonard Rossiter

Three Centuries from now, three men from the West shall be given charge of a Little Lady

You may well be disappointed by the contents of this box

The Codge Giant

Constructed in 1867 by **Lillian Billion** as a memorial to her late husband William, this tile gentleman was one of the last follies to be built in the area.

Standing over **30 feet** in height, he towers over the Codge countryside. During the Second World War, the Framley Regiment planned to conceal themselves in the base and use the tower as a disguise to frighten off enemy invaders.

Above, the brick monument and right, Billiam Million the Willionaire.

Jolly Follies

There's no better way to leave your mark on your surroundings than building a huge version of your own arse in stone. In the olden days, however, people built **follies** like the ones below.

If you've ever passed by Wripple on the B108, you may have noticed the C19th tomb of **Sir Reginald Bostrom**, the eminent Victorian scientist.

The top, which is in a state of constant suspension six feet above the base is thought to have been an earlier C18th addition.

A Room with that View

Rope

Of all the follies built on or about Framley, the finest must be the one built in Whotten Plodney by local entrepreneur and habitual gambler, **Sir Roberick Rope**.

In 1784, Rope made a drunken bet with **Dolan Snint**, a friend from London, that the view they had both recently enjoyed from the **East side window** of Rope's Whotten Plodney country house was also visible from the **West side window**.

It was decided that if this were not the case when Dolan visited the following week, that Sir Roberick would pay his usual forfeit and go around the world in 80 days.

Within seconds of returning home and throwing open the curtains, a sobering realisation hit Sir Roberick. Although his West window gave a commanding view over the church and village, all he could see from the East side window was a field and a goose and a bucket.

Not one to be outdone in a wager, Rope immediately ordered some local workmen to set to work in the eastern field, building an **exact 1:1 scale replica** of the landscape visible from the West window. In order to add credibility to the scene, Sir Roberick employed **an actor friend** to stand from dawn until dusk at the top of the replica church tower and be seen "admiring the view".

Snint

Unfortunately, four days later, the actor found himself drunkenly engaged in a bet with a friend about the view from his church. In what seemed no time at all, the workmen were at it again, labouring day and night to replicate the tower's Westerly view on its East side for the benefit of the boastful thespian. The project included a perfect copy of Sir Roberick's House and an entire troupe of actors to populate it.

When Snint arrived at Rope's house the next day to inspect the 'identical' view from Sir Roberick's East window, he was met with the sight of an **actor dressed as himself** waving back at him from a duplicate house 300 yards in the distance. The illusion was ruined and the bet was lost.

The seemingly endless set of replica **views** still stands in Whotten Plodney to this day, making it hard to tell exactly when you have left the village. *Do please allow plenty of time for your journey.*

C M Y K

tached nice and tight to the rising main with a branch tee connector or
opend. Nice one Sausages.

a food processor, whizz up your garlic, tomatoes, chilli, ginger and
arjoram with a good bosh of salt. Wallop the chicken lumps into a snug-
ting casserole-type pan, and add the schlock from the processor. Reduce
half innit.

hile this is binging away, screw the ballcock to the end of the arm. Don't
orry, it's not as easy as it sounds! The rubber diaphragm should be cosy
ith the Torbeck valve. Word.

move the bird/veg/herb combo from the pan and fry off the onion and
lery until golden or brown. Sweet as.

ally, lag the pipes with mineral wool mat or slit lagging (use 25mm or
gger if you're rocking with 15mm pipes). Check the back plate and the
rvice valve, and snap the polylid back into place. Easy now.

ason generously, and serve with a simple sexy crunchy lusty bouncy salad
57). Storming stuff my gorgeous chinas.

ere you go – a smashing summer dish, and a new cold water tank.
imba clart!

y this: White fish instead of chicken. Blimey.

this: Threaded inserts can be added to the Torbeck valve if you get a load
my old mate 'water hammer'. Chirpsing.

400g chicken (hen or cock)
1 branch tee connector or stopend
2 onions and/or chopped
1 part-2 ball arm
1 head of celery (hair removed)
1 ballcock (manufactured to BS 4213
WRAS approved)
4 cloves garlic, finely smashed
22mm straight connector
6 vine-bronzed tomatoes, surprised
Torbeck valve (with rubber diaphragm
1 red chilli, seeds
1 snap-on polylid
1 bye-law 30 kit
1 eye-sized piece of ginger, skinned
1 back plate
1 22mm compression tank service val
marjoram (pretty flowers)
mineral wool mat or slit lagging (min
a right load of old clothes

JOB NAME:	JAMIE'S LOFT
JOB NUMBER:	PEN00546-1
CLIENT:	PENGUIN BOOKS
CONTACT:	KATHARINE BOLLAR

The Story of Señor Ïh

Ask a Framley child 250 years ago what they like to watch and they'll tell you Señor Ïh every time. And they'll tell you the same thing today.

These puppet entertainments in their gay green-and-yellow striped tents were brought to Framley in the 11th Century by the Catalan **Pilgrim Butchers**, and were originally intended as daily marketplace sausage advertisements for the Meatmakers' Guild. The shows would have been strictly adults-only, and understandably so, as sausages are still officially classified by DEFRA as The Devil's work.

However, over the years, as the story grew more violent, children naturally grew more interested in Ïh. By c.1675, the appeal of the raw sausage noose of puppet justice was undeniable. It is around this time that the traditional narrative was established that we know and tolerate today. Soon the character was well on its way to its current position as the 8th most popular of all time.

PART ONE: The anarchic performance begins with the **Baby** figure painfully giving birth to a screaming **Señor Ïh**. By using circular breathing, the **Puppeteer** may carry on the terrible sound for twenty minutes or more until the end of the first half is reached.

PART TWO: Much of the rest of the plot is taken up with a discussion between **Señor Ïh** and the **Seventeen Architects** in which they debate at length the precise technicalities of building an extension onto the Ïh residence.

In the final scene, **Señor Ïh** performs an unsteady tap dance whilst holding a lit candle. The puppeteer or **Ïh-wrangler** is unable to see properly and the surrounding tent usually catches fire, obscuring any efforts to bring the story to a conclusion.

The **widow of the puppeteer** will then put out the smouldering remains with her tears in a live-action scene whilst dressed as **Judith**, the puppet widow of **Señor Ïh**. Finally, a ten-gallon stetson is passed around for the children to climb into.

Performances of the Ïh Play wer temporarily outlawed in the 18t Century after a rogue Señor Ïh at May Fayre in St Eyot's sproute legs and strolled amongst th audience, finally following a unfortunate young woman to he home where it *"dwell'd neath th good lady's bed, maintaining he underpotte at temperatures c unnatural high scalde"*

[from *The Conjectural Diary c Bernard Pepys*, 1709

The 2-inch lead replica of Señor Ïh, which is h swallowed by the puppeteer to produce the lilt hacking quality of the character's voice.

Illustrations cut out from Galsby Manuscript, Ï in Framley Museum Archive.

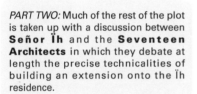

The Perineum Club

It's scientifically impossible to imagine now but in the days before *Countdown* was invented, when Carol Vorderman was just a twinkle in her great-great-great-grand-milkman's glass eye, men of the Framley past had to find other ways of entertaining themselves. I know! Unfathomable, isn't it!

Anyway, **Lord Henry Bionic** *(see box over there)* was one such men. In 1798, growing bored with the lack of decent dictionary-related television quiz shows (and who wouldn't have?), he founded a gentleman's club and he found it on the very outskirts of Framley itself. Bionic named it **The Perineum**

Club after his beloved nanny, Mrs Perineum Club.

In partnership with his erstwhile drinking partner, **Sir Itchibald Figgywicke** *(see the exact same box over there)*, Lord Henry established a club dedicated, in his words, to *"Bacchanalian pursuits, deadly sins, debauchery, vice, bombing, running, heavy petting and mischief in all its variant forms"*.

Initiation into the brotherhood was no picnic (the Picnic Initiation having been abandoned early on for being too easy). It was commonly said that in order to join, one needed to be *a relative of God, and not by marriage neither"*. Would-be members needed to pass a series of tests, including drinking a gallon of tar, flying, and stealing a policeman's job.

After almost fifty years of near-satanic excess, the Perineum was finally **closed down** in 1846, in the wake of *"a singular incident"* (The Chutney Herald).

The plaque from above the door of the Perineum Club was often pressed to service as a makeshift weapon or, in the winter months, a sledge.

On the 14th of March, Figgywicke, having spent a fortnight locked inside his office attempting intercourse with a stuffed bear, emerged into the dining chamber in a state of disarray. He pounded the table, called for order, declared himself too sexy for his hat, and the club was immediately consumed by flames.

The site of the original Perineum Club is now home to a popular *Harvester* restaurant which is not thought to be on fire at the time of writing according to their head office.

The founders

Lord Henry Bionic was a laudanum-crazed idiot and famed poet of the Romantic era/sort.

He sported a brass face after losing his own in a duelling incident, and a wooden leg which he had won in a bet.

Sir Itchibald Figgywicke MP was elected in 1792 as Tory M of P for the constituency of Framley & Plinth.

Figgywicke held many prominent cabinet positions including Secretary of State for Potatoes, Beatmaster General and Chief Pleasurer to King George III.

The two wastrels met when Figgywicke laid his cloak over a **puddle** to enable the safe passage of a lady *"with whom he quite fancied his chances"*. As he bent over to retrieve his apparel, the MP was startled to witness Bionic emerging from the puddle with the cloak on his head.

Although they became firm friends, Sir Itchibald never truly forgave Lord Henry for this act of ostentatious showmanship.

Tale of horror

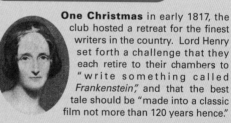

One Christmas in early 1817, the club hosted a retreat for the finest writers in the country. Lord Henry set forth a challenge that they each retire to their chambers to *"write something called Frankenstein",* and that the best tale should be "made into a classic film not more than 120 years hence."

Four days of lonely toil later, Mary Shelley had completed her manuscript. Convinced that victory was hers, she entered the snooker room, eager to present her opus.

She was greeted by blank expressions. The group had failed to inform her that, five minutes after the initial task had been set, the challenge had been changed to "showing your bum", and that her husband, Percy Bysshe, had already achieved an unassailable lead.

Framley's Mayors through the age

The heart and soul of a town is often said to reside in the shoes of its Mayor. Here we take a moment and look back through history at some of the memorable men and women who have

Turn again...

In the annals of Framley mayors, the most notorious is probably **Dick Fearnley-Whittingstall**. In the 15th Century, Dick walked into Framley with his pet Puss-in-Boots over one shoulder and a spotted red-and-white hanky filled with all his earthly possessions (mainly blue curacao and overproof rum) over the other.

Dick had walked over two hundred miles on the promise that the streets of Framley were paved with paving stones, which he believed he would be able to sell on the lucrative Dutch slab market. Unfortunately, the town's thoroughfares were at that time paved with gold, due to a controversial road-widening overspend, and Dick left town a broken man.

Outside the city walls, he sat down dejected and consumed the provisions in his spotted kerchief. Suddenly he heard a voice in his head intoning the famous words:

"Turn again, Fearnley-Whittingstall, thrice Mayor of Framley..."

Dick replied with the even more famous words:

"The Mayor is not for turning..."

and received a huge imaginary round of applause.

Within minutes he was asleep face down in a ditch, where he drowned, leaving Framley in a state of anarchy for three mayoral terms from which it has never fully recovered. To add insult and injury to injury, without Dick in town, Admiral Fitzcracker's daughter Mary lived her life alone and died a spinster librarian, never having given birth to their children Zuzu and Clarence, and the Building and Loan went bust.

A 19th century engraving, showing a visit to the town market b Simon Smith, the Amazing Dancing Mayor.

It's only money!

Mayor **Stephen Popmonster** (1956 - 1958) was th most contentious spendthrift ever to hold the office His budgets, often delivered years after the event an covered in tea and drawings of skeletons, taxed th greatest financial brains of the age. Famously, one c his account ledgers was bought by the Pur Mathematics department of St Hilda's, Oxford in 196 (the theorem known as **Popmonster's Parado** derives from studies of the mayor's estimates fo Maxpax coffee machine refills 1957 - 58 and is sti unproven).

The **pie chart** to the below is the result of forty year disentangling of records of Framley Council spendin from the third period 1956 and gives some idea c Popmonster's magnificent achievement.

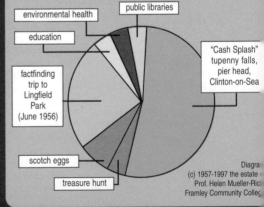

environmental health

public libraries

education

factfinding trip to Lingfield Park (June 1956)

"Cash Splash" tupenny falls, pier head, Clinton-on-Sea

scotch eggs

treasure hunt

Diagra
(c) 1957-1997 the estate
Prof. Helen Mueller-Ric
Framley Community Colleg

Sir Edward Duke
1920 - 28

A most remarkable character. Dandy, stage escapologist, gentleman thief and noted master of disguise. Duke was famously deposed by his sworn enemy the Pink Phantom in a military coup in 1926.

After two years of public hand-to-hand fighting at civic events, the mayor was shot in the head by the Phantom, who removed his mask to reveal he had been Sir Edward all along.

Sir Edward received a standing ovation from the crowd and remained in power for two more years before returning to his native Switzerland.

"Mad Dog" Alan Evans
1934

At his inauguration, Evans promised to be tough on crime "at the source". Four weeks later he had personally shot and killed every one of the town's criminals, three council members and a man who had given him a parking ticket before turning the gun on himself and retiring.

The Very Hungry Mayor
1966
by Eric Curlywurly
£4.99 Moth Books Hardcover
ISBN 0-7181-4579-8

Billygoat McKenzie
1961 - 62

Mental illness dogged McKenzie's short term in office. Within weeks it was clear that the mayor's love of opening ceremonies had overtaken all his other administrative priorities.

McKenzie ordered the building of hundreds of new leisure centres, supermarkets and needless civic amenities, including a Museum of Tramps and an "avenue of minarets" along the diving board at the municipal baths.

He was overthrown in a mutiny following a council meeting when councillors were not allowed to speak until McKenzie had tied ribbon over their mouths and cut it.

Mayor Brian Rose
1555 - 1655

On the fateful day he was instated, Mayor Rose pricked his finger on a spinning wheel and fell asleep for a hundred years and a day, a common hazard in the sixteenth century. Despite valiant attempts, the council were unable to wake him and a state of emergency was declared throughout the land.

Though briars and thorns grew round the civic administration department, only the kiss of Richard Craddock, a deputy mayor who was pure in heart was enough to wake him from his slumber.

They married and lived happily ever after in the Director of Housing's gingerbread office.

Yokami Fujimoto
1989 - 90

Winner of a phone-in competition on Tokyo radio to become Mayor of Framley for a year, 14-year-old Yokami made wide-ranging changes to the town.

At her request, Framley was renamed "Jelly Twiggy Jelly Town" on all maps and signage, the Magistrates' Court was redecorated with stickers of brightly coloured cartoon kittens, and £14m of taxpayers' money was diverted into building a giant Rock 'n' Roll Robot.

Ellery Quints
1950 - 54

Quints, a compulsively clean man, overruled his advisors by allocating 100% of his four year services budget to public hygiene.

Dustmen were given sweeping new powers of stop-and-search, forcing their way into people's homes, and following them round aggressively with unwanted drinks coasters and stain removal tips.

Quints encouraged skyscraping wages and extensive benefits packages for bin men, attracting many high profile, overqualified people to the profession, including HRH The Duchess of Kent and Frank Sinatra.

The Legend of Martin Degville

There can't be a schoolchild left alive who doesn't know the story of dashing highwayman **Martin Degville** and his epic ride from Fracton to Effing Sodbury in 1734.

History suggests that, in an attempt to escape government agents wishing to inspect his expenses claims, the fabled Dandy character rode the 8-mile journey in a little over six months. Anyone travelling the route today will see just why it took him so long. In every village on the way, he opened a franchised branch of the Highwayman gastropub chain, each bearing a plaque *"Martin Degville Slept Here - Join The Heritage Trail"*.

Legend tells that Degville made a name for himself on the lawless highways of Britain, stealing from the short and giving to the tall. Mounted on his faithful steed **Sputnycke**, Degville would redistribute wealth using a complex series of height charts and algorithms, some of which are kept in the Framley Museum's Special Documents Department to this day, today (14th March). *(Details correct at time of going to press).*

As well as newspaper reports and legal docume Framley Museum also has one of Ma Degville's original horseskin tape meas and a hemp post-it note from his pantry d reminding him to buy some more milk.

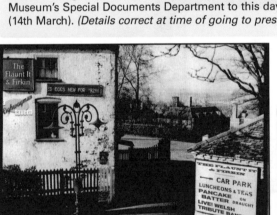

The Flaunt It And Firkin, just outside Whotten Plodney is probably the most celebrated of all Whotten Plodney's Degville-related inns. It is still used as a base by drug dealers, ram raiders and benefit fraudsters - the modern day equivalent of the romantic highwaymen of olden days!

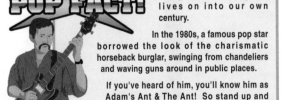

POP FACT!

The spirit of Martin Degville lives on into our own century.

In the 1980s, a famous pop star borrowed the look of the charismatic horseback burglar, swinging from chandeliers and waving guns around in public places.

If you've heard of him, you'll know him as Adam's Ant & The Ant! So stand up and deliver, it's nothing to be scared off.

Train robber

It can be hard to distentanglangle the man from the myth, but one myth is definitely true. Contemporary document sources confirm Degville's involvement in the so-called **"Great Train Robbery"** of 1727, the horrific incident in which the country was robbed of the invention of the steam train

After coming wig-to-wig with Degville in a bungled highway holdup, **George Morrisonson**, the Engineer Laureate, was so traumatised that he forgot how to invent railways. It wasn't until almost a hundred years later that George Stephenson (no relation) was struck on the head by a toy locomotive while sitting under an apple tree and came up with the idea of trains and tracks and the Tannoy public address system, ironically depriving highwaymen of their main source of income forever.

Here are some good old coins

There really is nothing like a coin, they* say, unless it's some old stamps or a vintage 1964 injection-moulded washing up bowl! So let us take a look at some of the rusty money that makes up over 80% of the museum collection, fascinating young and old alike, capturing everyone in the glamorous spell of coins...

* Barry and Lauren Clabtree of the Framley Numismatic, Philatelic and Washing Up Bowl Collectors' Guild

SESTERTIALIDOCIOUS
Roman, Circa AD144

The legendary *Sestertius Imperator*. A coin so valuable (and nourishing) that one of them would have fed a Roman soldier for life.

BAY-OF-PIGS SIXPENCE
GB, 1961

A commemorative coin issued to celebrate the nuclear brinkmanship of Kennedy and Kruschev, pictured head-to-head on the obverse. The coins were minted near the US Army test site on Bikini Atoll and rendered anyone with lots of loose change impotent. *"In the event of atomic attack,"* the warnings told us, *"hide behind a sixpence."*

HAND-MADE ROYAL FLORINS
English, 1973

The Royal Mint's work-to-rule in 1973 meant responsibility for manufacture of sterling coins reverted to the Royal Family. Princess Anne made these examples, hand-baked and decorated with SunMaid raisins for the eyes.

3fip GPO COIN
English, 1975

t of a brief merger
een the Royal Mint and
General Post Office.
is the second-class 13fi
ce coin, which, though
per, took slightly longer
ach your bank account.

Learn your new coins...

"There are eleven sevens in every four. Three fours is equal to an old sixpence, or new eight-sided twelvepenny bit. Twelve plus four plus four plus four plus four plus five, minus four is the new four, and that's almost the same as a groat. **It's that simple.**"

The Royal Mint

PRE DECIMAL "FOUR"
English, 1969

This experimental currency was introduced in 1969 but withdrawn within six months. Although the trial was short-lived, many people still remember the Public Information films screened to introduce the new coinage, and their catchy jingles and slogans *(left)*.

RARE PENNY
GB, 1915

imple miscalibration of the
ss at the casting plant caused
figure of Britannia on the
erse side of this run of
wardian pennies to be
aced by that of Popeye.

MAGNETIC SHILLING
GB, 1851

A sensation at the Great Exhibition of 1851, magnetic money was soon adopted as the Empire standard. All silver coinage was magnetised by the Mint, positively on the heads side, negatively on the tails, enabling tips and change to be attached conveniently to waiters' trays, cabbies' footplates or the metal corsets of prostitutes. In 1854, however, a mispressing of thousands of double-headed magnetic shillings led to the scheme being abandoned, after a spate of pocket-fires caused by rapidly spinning change.

20p COIN
UK, 1982

Launched in 1982 to promote The Thompson Twins' forthcoming single *Love On Your Side*, the twenty pence piece was an immediate hit, accepted by most major retailers. Originally intended purely as a promotional novelty, ver ten million of the giveaway coins were soon in circulation, threatening to eriously unbalance the economy and wiping out many people's life savings vernight. The looming financial crisis was only averted when Chancellor of the xchequer Geoffrey Howe went cap-in-hand to Alannah Currie. The single stayed in he UK charts for thirteen weeks, peaking at number 9.

The Framley Tales

If you went down to the woods today, but **200 years** ago you'd have had to bring a story with you! In 1806, spurred into action by the council's decision to turn the Molford greenwoods into a leisure centre, Molford academics the **Different Brothers** began their life's work, living in the forest and collecting all the traditional folk tales that lived there.

The tales they gathered had previously only existed in **oral form**, passed down the generations from mother's knee to daughter's knee. Now, for the first time, these simple folk yarns and traditional fairy stories would be published, allowing intellectual study of the form and cartoon animal re-enactments in colourful song and Difney DVD.

The brothers spent **five** years going from house to house in the rural community. Using gentle persuasive tactics and gifts, they would ingratiate themselves into the closed world of the greenwood household, then, as soon as dusk had fallen and the mother of the house was drunk, they would pin her to the floor and remove the stories from her skull using a drill and a pair of bellows.

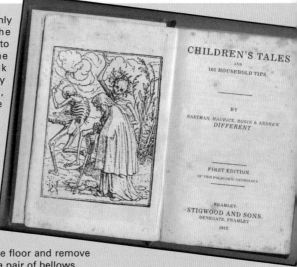

In **1812**, the brothers published the fruits of their painstaking labours; *Children's Tales and 101 Household Tips*. It was an instant bestseller, and was soon followed by *The Framley Legends* (1814), and three years later by *The Greenwood Stain Removal Goddess*. A compilation of all three books, published in 1820 became the most successful book ever to be published in the area, outselling *Lord Sockford's Summer Salads* and *The Bible* by a ratio of two to one.

The brothers' last work, an anthology of oral creation tales, *How This Book Became And Other Stories* (1828), was to be their last, and in 1832 they were all unexpectedly run over by a **boat** while crossing the upstairs landing of their Molford home. Their work, however, lives on, and it is hard to imagine how much poorer our cultural lives would be had the Different Brothers not decided to spend all those years in the woods tracking down other people's stories and stealing them.

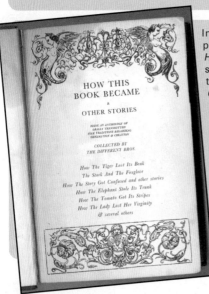

First edition frontispieces of *Children's Tales...* and *How This Book Becam*
Portraits (from top): Barry, Robin, Maurice and Andy Diffe

Telling the Tale...

Moth Books' series of traditional folk tales, first published in the 1960s, were many people's first introduction to the tales gathered by The Different Brothers.

The vigorous retellings of the stories and the beautiful oil painted illustrations only caused bedwetting in 15% of children, according to recently released government statistics, and the books were a great success, finding their way onto bookshelves all over the area whether people wanted them or not.

The books were printed locally at the Moth Books plant in Sockford right up until 1978. With the publication of **The Framley Examiner**'s first issue in March of that year, many people turned to newspapers instead and the market for the pocket-money hardback fairy tales evaporated. The devastating effect on employment in the area can still be felt today if you hold a seashell up to your ear.

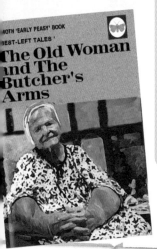

MOTH 'EARLY PEASY' BOOK
' BEST-LEFT TALES '
The Old Woman and The Butcher's Arms

The tales of the Different Brothers found a whole new unwilling audience thanks to *Les Editions Moth.*

' BEST-LEFT TALES '
The Disappointing Kettle
A MOTH 'EARLY PEASY' BOOK

' BEST-LEFT TALES '
Oleg and the Dancing Hats
A MOTH 'EARLY PEASY' BOOK

' BEST-LEFT TALES '
The French Connection II
A MOTH 'STAGE THREE' BOOK
FOR MORE CONFIDENT READERS

' BEST-LEFT TALES '
The Princess and the Pisshead
A MOTH 'EARLY PEASY' BOOK

' BEST-LEFT TALES '
The Queen's Tits
A MOTH 'EARLY PEASY' BOOK

' BEST-LEFT TALES '
The Gingerbread Scotsman
A MOTH 'EARLY PEASY' BOOK

' BEST-LEFT TALES '
Erkanmustafa
A MOTH 'EARLY PEASY' BOOK

The tigers were impressed by the old lady's new arms.

"I can make sausages, and mince, and pie filling in *half* the time," she said to herself.

"My tigers and I will never go hungry again."

' BEST-LEFT TALES '
Snow White, The Dwarf and the Other Six Dwarves
A MOTH 'EARLY PEASY' BOOK

◄ The Moth Books factory in Sockford employed almost 3,000 staff, producing over 40,000 metric gallons of fairy tales a week until its closure in May 1983.

A CDB Lithoplant operator in the control booth of the Moth Books turbine hall uses a Ranwell JS180 to increase the number of goblins in a story. ►

WHEELBARROW EXERCISE FOR ALL.
"The Foe of Lethargy"

This is a pastime of the greatest utility to the busy gentleman, as it gives the same results as would otherwise only be obtainable with a whole week of swimming or polo mallet tossing. The gentleman reclines whilst pushed in a barrow of considerable comfort. Exercise of the mouth is also displayed by the commands 'Stop!', 'Go!' and 'Faster!'. The wonder of the modern age. Encourages respiration and checks the ossification of the blood.

Price three week course £1 8 0

LADIES' SANITORIES
"Discretion an Imperative"

Linen curse flannels 4/6
Lockable nightgown 12/5
Wooden swaddling jockeys
(For gentle exercise) 8/6
'UNCLEAN' placards 2/6
Lengths of carefully poisoned bandage 2/6

BUTCHERS' OFFCUTS
(For the Needy)

Blood, urine, freshest melancholy.
Offal 0/2
Goat's Tails 0/1
Pig-Eye Porridge 0/1
Dog Gut 0/2
Braces of uncured crow 0/4
Rat crackling 0/1

CRAVEN'S
"CAREFUL CADDY"

Faith restored! Now the happy golfer need never forgo his tea or tee again.

Can be set to brew the perfect pot of Indian tea at intervals of 1, 2 or 18 holes.

There is a broad strap running along the top of the caddy that can contain up to 3lb of snuff.

Comes with pack of fifty tees.

Best make (The Maharajah) .... each 49/9
Second quality (The Marylebone) .... each 34/0
Cheapest quality (The Pardon-Me) ... each 0/3½

BERRYMAN'S PATENT DANCING SHILLING

Endless entertainment for ONE SHILLING. Mechanism comprises ingenious combination of clockwork and the Dark Arts.

One Dancing Shilling .... each 1/0
Two Dancing Shillings (Waltz) 2/0

CHILD'S POPPING WEASEL

The perfect accompaniment to nursery story telling.

Send unquiet children to sleep effortlessly with a tear in the eye and hair full of weasel innards.

Popping Weasel .... ½lb. 0/2 rice

LADIES' HEAVY VESTS.
(White Silk and Cast Iron.)
(unshrinkable, so-called.)

Low necks, metal sleeves .... 5/6   5/9 – 6/3
White merino, rust-resistant ...... 6/3   6/6 – 7/0
Silver trim, light flow .... 7/6   7/8 – 8/4

LUNCHEON HAMPERS.

Suitable for travellers, excursionists, policemen, escapologists &c. Each box contains 3 tins and will be found sufficient for a light luncheon when travelling. Suitable to be eaten with either a bread or Fenworthy's Patent Air Biscuits.

No. 1. Consisting of Pate, Opium and Crushed
Plum Pudding .... per box   1/6
No. 2.   "   Grain, Maize and Corn
.... per box   1/6
No. 3.   "   Cake, Tongue, Tonguecake
.... per box   1/6

DIGNITY BUREAU

This handsome, burr walnut bureau with exquisite Mother-of-Pearl detail, comprises honesty drawer, Bible well, collar press, moustache mirror, and cane hook. Comes complete with upright chair.

Gentleman's Bureau as described 2 19 5
As above with hair tonic dispenser 2 20 6

ENGLISH CHIMING CLOCK
("Old Bastard")

Size about 15 in . high, 12 in. wide, chiming bells on seconds, gongs on minutes, "cuckoos" on hours and small explosions at midnight £26 8 0
Ditto. Larger size, 10ft. high, 5ft. wide, small wooden characters enact play set in belly of whale every hour. Some coarse language £50 16 0
Shotgun £6 10 0

SUNDRIES & COLLECTABLES
From the Lands of the East

Elephant's tusk croquet hoops 3/6
Tiger Hide Top Hats 13/6
Servants (each) 1/2

RESTLESS SPIRIT STOVES.

This stove is th perfec accompaniment fo Camping, Races Picnics, Seance Regattas, &c.

Capacity 4 pint and one occupant o the spirit world.

Spirit likes: Egg Cut Ham, Pigeo Pie, Mayonnaise.

Spirit dislike Condiments, Roas Fowls, Sweet Sherry

Stove containing spirit 3/
(not available without spirit. Spirit lives in stove)

YOUTHS' BATMAN CAPES

3 button, Tan, Black Reindeer mask 3/
4 button, Black, Slate Gazelle mask 5/1

DUNKLEY'S PATENT PAPIER MACHE TEETH.

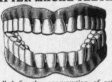

Unrivalled for the consumption of soft, d foodstuffs, these teeth will give hours of mer mastication. On softening, they can be dried in th oven and reused - giving a pleasant toasted arom
3 sets .... 2.

GUIDES TO DANCING.

How to Dance (Scott) .... 0.
How not to Dance (Scott) .... 0.
Crompton's Electric Boogaloo 0
Guide to dancing without music 1

NEW & POPULAR DANCES

Ball of the Belle 1/4	Man on my Face...............
Bid me Good Riddance . 1/6	My Horrid Hair 2
Dancing thru the Ceiling. 1/6	Sinking Boating Song.......
Drunk's Promise........... 1/4	They Love Eating Soil ... 3
Five Knuckle Shuffle..... 1/4	Two Lovely Broken Legs.
Garden of Manure.......... 1/4	When I was on Fire..........
Jolly Arsonist (The)....... 1/6	Whoft Tommy.................

UNPOPULAR DANCES

(The) .... 1/4 | 24 Hour Waltz ....

Pianofortes by Archibald Ricicle & Sons

Paris Exhibition 1900   **GRAND PRIX**   **Highest Award.**

PIANOFORTES, PARLOUR & GRAND.

No. I. THE BECHSBERG "LITTLE ANGELS" KLAVIER.

A compact upright piano of the smallest possible size. The tone is pleasing and the touch responsive.
Overstrung.
Complete iron framing.
Patent repeating action.
Ivory key.
One key only (middle "C")
Rosewood case.
Length, 1ft.
Width, 1ft. 2in.
Height, 3ft. 0 in.

Price 40 Guineas.

No. II. THE LEVIATHON.

A full-toned grand piano of responsive touch ar distinguished exterior. Twenty-one octaves of music, ten yards of astonishing length. A new system of construction renders the instrument indestructible.
Reinforced cast-iron framing.
Compass, 21 octs. A to A.
Patent hammer felts.
Under damper action.

Suitable for rooms of very large dimensions.

Length, 10yrds. 2ft. 2in.
Width, 4ft. 11in.
Height, 4ft. 2in.

Price 150 Guineas.

ORTSMAN'S QUARREL
*ccuracy is wayward and she reeks like a murdered slattern"
, your bowling is quite shit" —— (suitor expectorates upon sward of green)

VENUS ENSNARED
A popular lady once more thanks to Morrison's Bowling Toffees

GENTLEMEN'S TAILOR-MADE COSTUMES.

Pajama suits and Pajama Top Hats - The widest range of Empire styles.

Also somnolent formalwear and Midnight Canes for the well dress'd sleep-walker.

The Season Commences! - JUST IN: — Shooting sticks and rifles for sleep-hunting.
Designs available:
1. Burma Silk (to order only) 6/6
2. Oxford Stripe 8/0
3. Eton Twill 12/0
4. Flying Machines, Balloons and Boats 18/0
5. *The Muppet Show* 18/0

THE NEWEST SENSATION AT ASCOT, THE ETON BOATING SOCIETY &c.
'The Perambulator' Bicycle Suit.
Worn on a regular basis, the owner will benefit from increased health & vitality.
The unit can be controlled either from the shoulders, or by a passenger utilising the tweed handlebars mounted across the back.
The suit affords effective protection against the elements and when worn with overalls, renders the wearer absolutely proof against rain, dust or atmospheric wind. 37/0

MORRISON'S BOWLING TOFFEES

RRISON'S PATENT (*Stamped Quality*) Bowling Toffees are made only from toffees available. They last longer, much longer than the cheaper kinds of toffees, and are in all repects far superior to the many imitations which are ing offered for sale. They improve your aim and attract splinters, whilst ating the scalp through magnetism - thus encouraging hair growth.
☞ Ask for "MORRISON'S" *stamped quality Bowling Toffees.*

THE IRON TWAT.

With uncanny accuracy, this ingenious device will fire table tennis balls at the rate of twenty a minute in simulation of the popular ladies' parlour game.
Caution is advised as celluose balls may well ignite once fired.
Unique magnetic operation may cure baldness in all.
The Iron Twat (includes set of coloured lottery balls).... 148/6

"THE IMPERATOR" ONANISM CABINET

Separated by Decency - United in Joy

With cane hole (for the gentleman) each 30/10

With parasol hook (for the lady or 'gentleman') each 32/10

With brass or copper lectern and leather bound bible each 37/10

Chaff Guard each 3/3

e fastest and best known means of preserving h and relaxation Now the gentleman and the may perform The Solitary Vice side-by-side out the necessity of conjugal unpleasantries.
'Privacy and Discretion Imperative - Marital Harmony Assured"

LADIES' HAND CORSETS

r shaping of the feminine hand. Consists of ze wrist supports and whale bone thumb ghteners. Latest unbreakable fastenings from East. Delicate yet ruthlessly effective. plines unruly hands.
Hand Corsets........................3/6

E IMPERIAL AIR GUITAR

ow action, medium gauge air guitar for the rning musician. Never requires tuning. 13oz ght. Available in cherry red, rosewood or union

"Imperial"......................each 21/0
lacement strings..................each 0/4

"WINDFATHER"
OR PUFF DADDY.

The latest and most amusing indoor game yet devised. Players take turns to propel the elderly paper gentleman around the 'arena' with straws. Windfather............................ 33/-

CHILDREN'S BOOKS

Pub at   Sold at

Hentai (G.A.), Books of Adventure.—— With a Bee in a Jar. At Agincourt on a Walrus. Fighting the Women. The Dangerous Harpsichord. Um Bongo the Humble Redskin. An Unsatisfactory Lover. The Biggest Mindgame of them All. Oddd: Or Things That Have Happened. Tom Bola's Schooldays.. Fifty-two Stories for Boys and one story for Adults. A Merrie Tale of Robin Hood. A Miserable Tale of Robin Hood. Mr. Egg's Holiday (or How To Cook an Egg). Pugglecat the Dog. Boring Bible Stories. Little Lord Mundane. .... each   6/0   4/6
Mince (Edward), Little Garden of Erotic Nonsense ('Rubbish, Rubbish')..... 6/0   4/6
Legs (Mrs. C), Pussy Galore, A Story of the Princess Elizabeth. 3/6   2/7½

GENERAL INTEREST

Observer's Book of the Working Class. .. 30/0   22/6
Wah, (Rev. M.), Railway Battles........ 3/6   2/10
Costello (Elvis), The Diary of a County Gentleman..................... 5/0   3/9
Beeton (Mrs. Isabella), Household Slavery.......................... 3/0   2/5
Kingdon Brunel, (I), The Pop-Up Book of the Lord's Prayer; A Storytelling Miracle in Iron. 30/0   22/6
Leoni ; A tale of the Franco-Prussian War. By Top Cat. 4/0   3/0
Crinoline (Hon. Mrs.), The Prettiest Horse Of All. 2/0   1/6
Gray (Dr. Johann), Gentlemen are from Mars, Ladies are from Venus. 4/0   3/0

MAGICIAN'S EGG TRICK.

Invention of the Orient. A Magic Egg placed inside of the bag vanishes leaving only the most remarkable smell.
Bag may require washing.
Egg Trick.........each 1/2
Magic Eggs available from Magician's Farms.

ONK'S PATENT HAIR TONIC.

There was an old man with a beard, Who declared 'It is just as I feared, Four owls and a moose, Six Camels and the Lord Chamberlain Have all made their nest in my beard!'
E. Lear
reprinted by kind permission

Before   *After*
Illustrations have not been altered in any way.

Onks original hair tonic is the ONLY one recommended by the senior trichologists of Britain.
Results in minutes..... bottle 1/2

DUELLING BANJOES.
Settling the Gentleman's Dispute since 1811.

"Sir, you are a dolt, a nonce and a nincompoop!"
"Sir, you have impugned my honour. I demand satisfaction!"
Satisfaction redeemed with the Original and Best Duelling Banjo. Available as five string, four string or twelve-bore models, with or without safety catches.
The Standard..........................2/3
The Deadshot..........................2/3
The Livingstone.......................2/3
The Diplomat..........................2/3
The Ready Reckoner....................2/3
The Habakkuk..........................2/3

How We Used To Kill Each Other

In the **bad old days**, the public had far gristlier appetites than their modern day ancestors, the contemporaries of today like **you and me**.

From the 12th century thousands flocked to Denegate to witness the four o'clock executions, whether it was the despatch of the tax-evading lord of the manor or the last plummet of the starving old hag found **guilty** of stealing a grain of salt.

The Framley Executions

▲ People hanged by the stomach could take up to two weeks to die, and were usually rescued.

This gruesome daily spectacle attracted spectators from all classes, with top prices being paid for seats in the stands. **Mammy Tomms**, who kept the key for the private viewing boxes, was also the landlady of *The Old Sod*, a nearby tavern where the tumbrel would traditionally pause on the prisoner's last journey for a pint of best courage and a hangman's lunch.

After being led through the town followed by hearses and mourning coaches, the condemned would have a rope noosed around their neck. The rope would then be tethered to the ground in front of a cannon, into which the prisoner would be stuffed before being fired into the air.

The victims' heads invariably fell into the crowd where spectators would fight to grab relics, like an ear or a moustache. The bodies, thanks to careful ballistic calculation, usually landed in **Dead Man's Sudd**, a marshy slobland where the Arnhem Centre car park now stands.

Executions were a public spectacle until 1868, despite loud voices of objection, including a piece in *The Illustrated Thunderer* by Charles Dickens, who denounced the onlookers as "*foggy pillocks.*"

Another one bites the dust, this time by being hanged by the neck. This popular method of execution outlived many of its victims. ▶

These aren't very nice

It wasn't just public executioning that kept the sweary masses happy in the darkest days of a terribly long time ago. Contemporary accounts record many other brutal entertainments taking place in the town square. St Eyot's diarist **Seymour Prig** recounts a visit to the Swan Fights with his collar-boy, and his account of watching the Brass Band Baiting in Clinton Gardens remains a set text at GCSE. Taking advantage of the warmer weather following May Day, the square played host to Broken Knuckle Boxing, popular crowd-pleaser The Ladder Into The Sky, and the punitive spectacle of Death By Chocolate which always drew appreciative audiences from the outlying villages and clerical professions.

HORRID MURDER

Gruesome wood-carvings were as popular with salacious Victorians than the blockbuster bloodbaths of today are with Betamax enthusiasts.

This cut, by **Blockmore Sedgeley Buzzwish**, aqa 'Buzz,' depicts horsemaker John Stone in the act of murdering the artist's *"god-dreaded piggy little cistern of an odalisque"* of a wife, **Elizabeth Buzzwish**, and was for many years a popular Victorian t-shirt.

Stone's stomach-curling crime included sewing the victim's severed head back on to the body with yachting twine and "sailing" her round the room until the police arrived.

Sockford Assizes

he **Victorian legal system** operated on several evels: the Magistrates and Petty Sessions were the ost trivial, meeting in pubs and horse-troughs; then ame the Quarter Sessions, which dealt with more erious offences, such as thuggery and buggery; and, t the top level, meeting once or three times a year out never twice) were the Assizes.

record of the **Assizes** from 1849 and 1868 give ome idea of the crime and punishment meted out by ur grumpy and wonderful ancestors.

KFORD SUMMER ASSIZE, 1868

	ENCOURAGING A WOMAN TO PARTICIPATE IN A GENTLEMAN SANDWICH	DISCHARGED
ELWYN BELWYN	SOLITARY RIOTING AT CHUTNEY-LE-BASIL	5 YRS TRANSP.
MARIE-RICHARD PUY	COUNTERFEIT MOUSTACHE AT SOCKFORD	14 YRS PENAL SERV.
JAMES WANNABIES	BURST HORSE	18M SOFT LABOUR
MINIATURE WILLIAMS	IMPERSONATING A RAPIST	ACQUITTED
HENRY CLOCKSPROD	POSSESSION OF IMPOSSIBLE HEDGE MAZE	PENAL SERV. LIFE
EMINEM WILSON	STEALING £1-2-6D OF MUCK AT STREPSILHAM	12M DIRTY LABOUR
'RAMSAY THE PONCE'	UNNATURAL OFFENCES & NEWSAGENCY	LUNATIC
JOSIAH BASTARDASTER	ATTEMPTED MURDER OF TOP HAT	DEFERRED
PETTIGREW MILLIFOLD		

OCKFORD WHITSUN ASSIZE, 1849

	DISGUSTING A POSTMISTRESS AT RUBMY	10 YRS TRANSP.
DR ANONYMOUS BOOTLACE-PERSPECTIVE	ATTEMPTING TO FLY	RESERVED
FLOYD BIZARRE	STEALING & DRIVING AWAY A HAYSTACK	10MINS HARD LABOUR
WILLIAM WILLIAM WILLIAMS	STOLE UNDERWEAR FROM SIMPLETON	APPLAUSE
PRINCE ALBERT	ATTEMPTED RAPE OF GOSLING AT POND FARM	5 YRS TRANSP.
EBENEZER PINCHPENNY	COME-HITHER LOOKS	STANDING IN CORNER
SPEARMINT MCRHINO	CURSING LIKE IRISH LABOURER	18M MOUTHWASH
PERSISTENT WALTON	GENTLEMANSLAUGHTER	BOLLOCKING
BRUT OILS	SAWING A LADY IN HALF AT URLING	350 YRS PENAL SERV.
MORTLAKE CANASTAFORD	DRUNK AND FULL OF FARTS	DEFLATED BY FORCE
SEXTANT BELABOURBY-BENZ	UNSEEMLY BALLADEERING	12M SILENT LABOUR
GERONTIUS LOUD	ASSAULT AND VINEGAR AT CRISPFORD	DEATH
CHARLOTINE IRONCLAD		

WINTER GARDENS - CLINTON

A GRAND SCIENTIFIC & MUSICAL DISPLAY OF

DEAD DOGS

Lent for the occasion by the PARISH COUNCIL of CLINTON

THURSDAY EVENING JANUARY 19 1885

Sir Coderick Fillet, Bart., M.P., in the chair

Messrs. BURA and HARDWICKE will exhibit their OWN RENOWNED collection of

ODDMEN & FANCY-FACES

CAPTURED from towns and villages NO LESS THAN FIVE MILES from the resort of Clinton

For your DELIGHT and WONDERMENT , there will be a public display by

PROF. ALBERTBEALE STEEPLECOCQUE

of his much admir'd STOPPED CLOCK, that doth misquote the correct time
on one thousand, four hundred and thirty-eight occasions in one single day

Mr Excelsior Melon's

FREEK-OUT

by Royal Appointment

Rear Admiral Sir Roderick Hull and his One-Man

ANTIPODEAN AVIARY

will be Recreating The Seasonal Birdsong Of Brisbane in its entirety,
presenting a Magic Lantern rendering of the Story of the Kookaburra
and introducing his own most pugnacious bird, The Emu.

THE GUARDIAN OF

MISS MILDRED HUFF

HAS GIVEN HIS KIND CONSENT TO HER DEMONSTRATING A RECITATION FROM THE BOOK OF LEVIATHON
CHAPTER SEVENTEEN VERSES 1 - 248

Admission :— Members, ? ; Re-Members, 2s. 6d. ; Family Tickets to Admit Fifty, 10s. 6d.   Doors open at 6.30 ; Commence at 7 o'Clock.

The visiting of this EXHIBITION has been proven to STIMULATE HAIR GROWTH in minors by utilising the powers
of MAGNETISM and has recently been EXHIBIHIBITED before THE CROWNED HEADS of EUROPE.

1885

The Clinton Winter Gardens often played host to displays of curiosities which would draw gawkers from miles around. In 1876, John Merrick,
famous Elegant Man was exhibited here, and fifteen years later, Whoft chemist Graham Curie used the Winter Gardens to demonstrate the first
practical uses of the new substance "plasticene" to an astonished scientific community by making a coil pot and a really long snake.

A Grisly Tale of Murder!

In the ninethteen century, the foggy streets of Framley were not a safe place to be after dark! For these streets were the stalking ground of the legendary, larger-than-life Dickensian character known as **"Jack The Rapist"**.

No matter how many witnesses there were to his grisly deeds, he was never identified. As dead prostitute after dead prostitute piled up on the police station doorstep, it seemed to many people that this colourful figure would evade detection forever.

And those people were right! For even today, the true identity of this grand old English eccentric has yet to be established, making this murder mystery just as popular now as it was in Jack's own day.

'ou'd like to have a go at solving the crime, Framley police keep an incident room ffed 24-hours a day in the Victorian Framley exhibit in the basement. If you have y evidence or opinions, or would just like to try on a police helmet, do drop in.

A rapist's impression of Jack The Artist. In his six year career, Jack raped and murdered 11 dockside prostitutes and an Aunt Sally from a travelling fairground. It was said at the time that he would *"go for anything with a pipe in its mouth"*.

The Hult for Jack

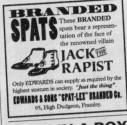

Jack The Rapist's reign of terror did not go unopposed. Hot on his heels was a most worthy adversary in the form of **Inspector Jack Challingham** of Framley Murder Squad. In the twenty years that he spent investigating the case, Challingham never wavered from his fervent assertion that *"no-one is above suspicion"*.

Insp. Jack Challingham

Framley gaol was soon heaving with suspects, including four of the dead prostitutes themselves and the County Coroner who, Challingham insisted was *"up to his damnable armpits in whore blood"* when arrested.

The accusations went right to the top of British society. Bearded playwright George Bernard Shaw was arrested twelve times on suspicion of being Jack The Rapist - and once for being the author of all Shakespeare's plays - and Prince Albert only escaped accusation by proving, in a demeaning experiment, that he was allergic to prostitutes.

Everyone loves a good murderer, and Jack soon became something of a celebrity, as popular as David Beckham is today.

Newspaper advertisements from the time show a burgeoning trade in Jack memorabilia, catering to a public hungry for toys and novelties tied in to his crazy antics. Framley Museum has the world's largest collection of related antiques and curios, but someone had leant a mop against the inside of the door of the storeroom and our photographer couldn't get in. Enjoy.

Jack the Cult

Funwood Treasures

If you'd been alive a hundred years ago, like I told you earlier in this book, then you might have been able to visit the brand new theme park at Clinton although you might not have been able to read this book.

A response to the growth of popular puritan-based entertainment of the time, **Funwood Treasures** was announced to the newly emerging tourist trade as the first self-contained leisure complex in the world. And what a first self-contained leisure complex in the world!

How it all began...............

In 1877, whilst walking over the cliffs above Clinton seafront, local entrepreneur **Ahundred Thompson** conceived a novel idea for an health spa and amusement area. By 1878 Thompson had bought a large clifftop plot of land and offered £1 of his own money (a small sum at the time) as a prize to anyone who could design a *"complex of tiny baths for the poor and unpleasant"*.

Architects were slow to take up on the challenge, but **Georgibald Bee**, designer of Fracton's 50 inland lighthouses, eventually put forward a proposal that was accepted. Building began in 1883 and was completed three years later on a Thursday.

The public opening of the health baths was an unmitigated shambles, with the entrance hall collapsing as soon as the supporting ribbon was cut by the presiding dignitary. Happily a small group of builders trapped inside the fallen building reported later that the main pool was both *"temperate and delicious"*.

Undeterred by this minor setback, Thompson returned to his draining board and began to realise the second stage of his dream.

The clifftop baths, as pictured at the time. Notice the steam-heated water flowing upwards to fill the indoor pools.

Opening in 1896 **Funwood Treasures** was a far more successful offering than the spa, comprising over a hundred of Thompson's specially designed *"Rides and Diversions for All"*

Business gradually picked up and, at the turn of the century, the park was greatly redeveloped and adapted, making it into one of the area's most popular areas.

Early Attraction

Thompson's remarkable achievement boasted many firsts, not least of which were the *Kinetic Chariots,* which many believe to be the world's earliest recorded dodgems or bumper-cars.

Powered entirely by steam, the miniature cars would swerve around a smoggy overcrowded arena scoring every time they bumped into one another, whilst an attendant, worth four points, lit the way for each chariot with a red lamp.

All fairs thrive on the sound of fear, and nothing at the park drew more screams than the *What the Butler Earns* machine. After a go on this device many ladies had to regain their composure with a steadying ride upon the mighty iron *Ferris Corset*.

In the *Crazy Household* visitors could enjoy the loopy spectacle of a home without servants, gasping at such sights as the woman of the house attempting to slice a loaf of bread with a parasol, and the patriarch trying to clean his own shoes with rat poison.

Most popular of all though was the innovative horse-drawn roller coaster *'Giddy Up',* which carried its passengers over a small incline in converted beach huts, before depositing them safely in the sea.

Mr Moony & Mrs Spinner, *pictured here on the Main Promenade,* became the two mascots of Funwood Treasures from the 1920s onwards.

The role of Mr Moony was traditionally taken by the reigning Miss Clinton, the mask obscuring her face a fitting punishment for having dared be quite so arrogantly beautiful.

Today we know them as the late Morecambe and the not quite so late Wise but before they became enormous they made their livelihoods performing at Funwood Treasures.

The tiny **Eric Bartholomew & Ernest Wiseman,** as they were originally known, delighted all that happened not to tread on them by mistake.

Spinner's Spinning Spikers were immensely popular with children who could send their parents down the chute to a sharp end should they find themselves tiring of the park.

The sound of screams emanating from the room would often attract huge crowds of baying infants and hungry dogs.

Funseekers with a sweet tooth would have enjoyed local specialities Candy Fluff, Mouthstoppers, Toffeesprouts or Acid Coughs.

Those with a savoury tooth were forced to make do with **Gravy Rolls**. Traditionally served gravy-side-down with a handful of Spinner's Special Sauce, one bite was enough.

The Boring Twenties

Better than Funwood Treasures

The **Experience of Being at Funwood Treasures Experience** is now open at Framley Museum. You too can pay an old-flavoured shilling and have a go or even some goes on the rides gone by.

Using the latest technology combined with state of the art subliminal suggestion you can actually *be* in the past! You won't believe your eyes ever again.

£9.50 for adults, £8.50 for children.
Please warn staff of any food allergies.

Where are they now?

Originally built on the clifftop at Clinton, Funwood Treasures gradually fell victim to the **raw power of the sea**.

Over the years ride after ride tumbled into the waves below, much in the same way that the designer of the attraction, Ahundred Thompson, had done six days before the construction of the theme park was completed.

Sometime over the last three years the entrance itself has finally succumbed to the crumbling land and the entire grounds are now resting on the seabed below.

"Now it's underwater it's more popular than ever," revealed manager, Peter Jeffries. "Attendances are down," he bubbled.

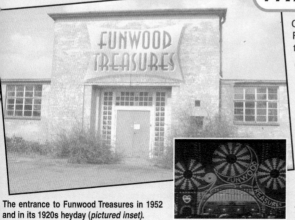

The entrance to Funwood Treasures in 1952 and in its 1920s heyday (*pictured inset*).

The Fluff Revolution

Until reasonably recently, the fluff industry played an important part in shaping Framley's economic growth.

Initially used for bedding, novelties and cloud manufacture, the quest for a ready supply of cheap power led to the development of ways of milling and mining of this seemingly inexhaustable substance. In 1632, the first fluff mine and mill were opened in 1639.

Mining

The mines, or *fluffieries*, were traditionally constructed on flat plains with a network of tunnels, often billions and billions of metres long, dug deep beneath. Excess fluff produced by the mills *(see opposite)* would then be buried by the miners, starting from the surface and working backwards to the pit's end.

A typical miner would have earnt the equivalent of a day's wages in today's day and age each day. Working hours were considerably longer than hours are now, however, and days could drag on for what seemed like days.

The working conditions within the mines were incredibly poor, with a high risk of fluff-related diseases such as *pneumoflufficosis*, a grim condition that meant many miners spent their evenings at home, doubled over, trying to cough up a massive hairball.

Safety measures were introduced in the mid C18th to lessen the daily intake of fluff on long shifts, miners being advised to work until the layer of fluff on their collars was the size of a dead canary and then leave the pit for the day.

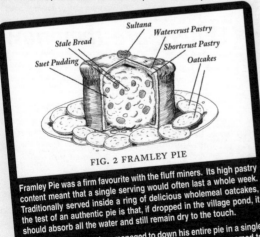

Sultana
Watercrust Pastry
Stale Bread
Shortcrust Pastry
Suet Pudding
Oatcakes

FIG. 2 FRAMLEY PIE

Framley Pie was a firm favourite with the fluff miners. Its high pastry content meant that a single serving would often last a whole week. Traditionally served inside a ring of delicious wholemeal oatcakes, the test of an authentic pie is that, if dropped in the village pond, it should absorb all the water and still remain dry to the touch.

In 1821, a foolhardy miner managed to down his entire pie in a single mouthful. The inn, 'The Dead Man' near Chutney, was so-named to commemorate his valiant effort.

Milling

Framley's *fluff mills* were responsibl for producing, gathering and refinin fluff for the town for ttp://www.fram leycollege.ac.uk/fluffmills/timeli e.html years.

Because fluff is generated naturall within large buildings, the mills wer overrun with fluff deposits whic could be gathere and put to use.

A miller gathering crude fluff in a *dustcan* like a stupid

The fluff produce by the mill wa employed to powe its machinery (i contravention o some scientific lav or other) and an excess would b buried by the fluf miners *(se opposite)*.

Framley owes muc of its prosperity to it excellent position o the fluff plain, a situation whic gave it an inbuilt advantage over les fluffy towns nearby, such as Clean Langley

The development of the Fluffing Jenny in 1798 revolutionised the process of refining **tidy fluff** from **crude fluff**.

Tidy fluff was essential for the industry, as it could be quickly and simply processed into crude fluff. It was also heavier and weighed less.

When the last of the fluff mills closed in 1964, Flidwell Nuc Power Station was constructed to cover the shortfall in po production. Because of this, fluff is no longer being sa buried and unseasonal fluff build-ups regularly occur in region, like Framley's notorious midsummer fluff storm of 1

HERE COMES DUSTY!
the Little Fluff Man

WHO'S that tapping at your window? Why it's Dusty - the fluff mascot - who ensures that every home in Framley is always full to the brim with fluff. Come rain . . . come pour, he'll be there. Just make sure you leave your fluff card in your window to show Dusty that you need topping up.

fluff FOR EVERYONE

ISSUED BY THE FRAMLEY FLUFF COUNCIL

Framley On Screen

The glamour of Hollywood has alwa' lived near Framley, as the *Framley C Screen* exhibit just behind the stairs the museum's Left Wing shows.

Framley's earliest recorded brush with the wonderful world of moving pictures came in 1888, when Doctor Rumbelow Whirlybird, a railway engineer and travelling entertainer, brought his *Peripatetic Penny Gaff* to the town.

Cramped inside a makeshift tarpaulin cinema, a bedazzled audience was treated to *"several demonstrations of the Wondrous Kinetoscope, wherein the MARVEL of the living image may deliver even the most audacious spectator an not inconsiderable BLOWING of the mind."*

Whirlybird's Kinetoscope took the form of a rotating tin containing a series of images which, when viewed through slits in the side of the cylinder appeared to *"dance and gambol as if imbued with the very vigour of life."*

Mr Whirlybird showed the stunned onlookers a series of 'kinematic strips' showing fully animated images of such sights as the letter L painted on a wall, and the Sphinx.

These vigorous sights drew gasps from his audience, but it was when the good doctor presented a kinetoscope image of a rotating kinetoscope going in the opposite direction that havoc broke out. Several women fainted and one confused soldier drew his pistol and put a bullet in his own mind.

The showman was hounded out of town by an angry mob, and his precious kinetoscope viciously smashed to pieces and kindly donated to the museum, where it can now be seen in the *Victorian Framley In Ruins* exhibit.

1888

The first commercial cinema in the area was the grand Sockford Polyhedron, opened in 1937 by strangely silent movie star Tommy Taplin.

Like picture houses all over the country that year, the Polyhedron showed film of the coronation of King George VI and Elizabeth VIII, although this led to confusion in the local press that the monarch had visited the town with a huge procession.

This was only the first of many incidents that seemed to indicate that the people of Framley were no more

The Golden Age

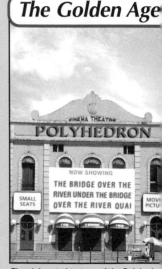

The elaborate frontage of the Polyhedrc was converted to Cinemascope in 1952.

ready for moving pictures than they had been in the age of Mr Whirlybird *(see left)*.

Contemporary press clippings from the St Eyot's Flugel reported, amongst other things, that a huge gorilla was tearing up Framley, that a tornado had blown away a little girl from Sockford, and that the hills above Whoft were alive with the sound of music.

When the 1969 moon landing was shown at the Wripple Mastodon, many of the audience believed that the surface of the moon was in the auditorium with them, and five people asphyxiated. One man had to be helped off the ceiling.

Eventually a series of short educational films were made explaining the concept of cinema, to preface each showing, presented by an enormous two dimensional version of Michael Redgrave, the size of a house who attended every performance from behind the cinema screen.

The impressive Polyhedron, designed in the modernist style by Gunther Wermin, still stands, although much of its stylish art deço interior now has formica nailed to it.

1984

The borough council found itself in hot water in 1984, when it built a bypass south of Wripple exclusively for the makers of the film *John Le Pram's The Magnificent Spy*. The road, which has not been used by any vehicle since, was used in a close-up shot of David Hasselhoff taking off a pair of sunglasses.

The project nearly bankrupted the borough, but councillors insisted that the road's starring role in the straight-to-video classic was excellent value publicity for the town. Hasselhoff's car can still be seen under a bridge on the unconnected bypass to this day.

Film overspend fiasco gets worse and worse

by TAUNTON MISHAP and "CHUCKLES"

FURIOUS WRIPPLE RESIDENTS took to the streets almost literally on Friday, when a group of 450 angry locals marched in protest against a new £92m bypass which is being built near the village for a scene in a big-budget spy film.

The loud annoyees insist that the inaccessible road, which does not join any other road, is running way over budget, and overstretching an already overstretched council overbudget.

The protest came in the wake of Framley Borough Council's announcement last week that dustbins could no longer be emptied daily, and that some buses would be reduced to running on two wheels.

"This is spiralling out of all sorts of control," flapped community leader Nelson Wilson. "We're demanding that the council take action against this sorry folly of vanity and insanity and inhumanity," he sang.

Highways Director Simon Trucks [HA! HA! LOOK AT THIS BLOKES NAME EVERYON] is reported to be hiding somewhere in a caravan.

Protest leaders warn that unless the project is abandoned, they will tear up the three-mile stretch of road and lay it at the doors of the town hall.

The film stars D a v i d Haselhof and is based on the bestselling thriller *John Le Pram's The Magnificent Spy* by John Le Pram.

O'Lorean's last bid

TROUBLED Belfast auto magnate Sean O'Lorean is to make an eleventh-hour plea to Framley Council to save his Sockford car plant.

The plant was intended to bring jobs to the area, but sales of the experimental Olorean 760 sports car have levelled off at between very few and none.

The car, which is made entirely of doors, has proved too futuristic for local tastes.

Despite the evidence, O'Lorean remains confident that people will learn to love his car.

"It's never been easier to enter or leave your vehicle. The revolving door behind the steering wheel is a particular favourite of mine."

The plant needs £30m to survive to the end of the week.

▲ The man Hosselhaff swinging from the spare tyre of his acacia tree.

))FRAMLEY EXAMINER))

)))) FRIDAY))))
WHAT THE BLOODY HELL IS GOING ON?
FRAMLEY EXAMINER

▲ *The Framley Examiner*, May 11th, 1984

1961

In 1961, gritty Sockford served as the backdrop for the cult rebel film *Barry Idiot*.

Filming took nine weeks, and the cast became familiar faces in the area. The star of the film, moody heart-throb Adam Daddy, was mobbed when he slipped into the Eggy Soldier café for lunch one evening, and his leading lady, smoky siren Marina Chardonnay, caused a near-riot by frolicking naked on the war memorial with a man in a panda suit for the film's infamous finale.

A BBC film crew supervise a scene from *Mambo* in German Cloud Avenue ▼

1978

The small screen has been no stranger to Framley neither.

In 1978, silver-tongued, smooth-haired actor-turned-hardman John Thaw and the young Delia Smith came to the town to film a hard-hitting BBC drama pilot about a tough, crime-solving milkman.

The series, *Mambo*, would have been a great success were it not for the unfortunate scriptwriting error that led to Thaw's eponymous detective being shot dead at the end of the pilot, leaving few opportunities for a full series.

Although the tape was later wiped by the BBC to make space for repeats, the show's cult following was enough to attract a legendary single coachload of Belgian tourists to the town in July 1989.

1926

The Molford Wo

Galham's Pig Butter
THE CHOICE FOR THE FAMILY

PRICE ONE PENNY

THE WORKING MAN'S CHAMPION

No. 244.

WEDNESDAY, 11TH SEPTEMBER, 1926

PORK SUNDRIES

ALL-NEW BAKELITE kitchen equipt., saucepans, double-boilers, ladles, butter corks, pork forks, &c. JOCKNEY'S BESPOKE, by telephone, FRAmley Exchange 664.

KNOTS of the world collection. Needs expert untangling. Could be worth a fortune but isn't at the moment. All offers considered. CODge 492.

ENGINEER'S VICE. Large, old but serviceable. Common shopgirls. Don't tell the wife. FRAmley 466.

VARIETY OF aromatic pipe tobaccos. Fish paste, nail varnish and tarpaulin. Sixpence a pouch. FRAmley 170.

GUESS MY NAME and win £20. Call Matthew Cuthbert Bland on FRAmley 874. Hurry! I'm running out of money.

OVERFLEXIBLE black and white cartoon 'mouse' with gloves and steamboat. Also cow/horse jugband and dancing trees. Causes slight uneasiness in stomach but once in lifetime opportunity. £2 2/6 Whoft 678

DELICIOUS engagement ring. Looks like a real engagement ring but melts in the mouth in moments. £12-2/6 WHOft 750

HALF A CHANCE

'TURN YOUR Family's Memories Into Thinly Chipped Potaoes!'. It's the salt & and & vinegar sensation of the Jazz Age! Satisfaction promised! Fram 198.

TRUMPET. One valve missing. Makes noise like Bix Beiderbecke being shot by Alexander Graham Bell. Fram 748. £2.

WELSH EGGGS. An egg encased in sausagemeat encased in a perfect shell. How do I do it? Just ask my mince hens! Contact Swansea Alan at Jones the Speciality Butcher, Chutney St Mary.

AUSTIN ONE, 1926, superior condition; with 'barking owl' klaxon horn, £14.4s.0d., apply WETHERMAN, Cutlery Cottage, Sockford.

LEAGUE OF NATIONS antemacassars, featuring grinning face of Woodrow Wilson. Also self-determination arm rests. Many to clear. FRAmley 380.

EXTRA STRONG bicycle clips. Secure legs firmly to side of bicycle ensuring inability to pedal. Essential. 3/6. FRAmley 544.

THE ZAMESI

COMPLETE SET of encyclopedias. All the encyclopedias in the world, collected together at last. Lifetime's work. Offers. FRAmley 141.

EVERLASTING Godstopper. Array of brass Bible brackets hold pages shut fast, avoiding danger of accidental religion. 4g. Wripple 713.

VOODOO pin cushion. Keeps pins tidy and causes untold suffering to other pin cushions. 1/8. FRAmley 655.

NAZI WAR MEMORABILIA. Boxes and boxes of flags, badges, shoes &c from the Third Reich (mainly 1941-45) Contact Professor Arthur Bostrom on Fram 446. Experiment successful. £8.

HIGH CHAIR. Approximately cloud level. I love you. FRAmley 056.

AEROPLANE cardigan. London to New York in next to no time and comfort. £2 11/6 each way. FRA0048

MANGLE, cast iron, fully functional with clockwork handle and tandem-style seats. The ride of your life. £2. WHOft 491

PROHIBIHIBITION

WILDLIFE PRESERVES. Zebras, hippos, giraffes and Asian Clouded Leopards all made into delicious marmalade. Surplus from global hunting expedition. Offers welcome. Contact WRIPPLE 821.

CHESTNUT BURNER, ready for Christmas work, £10. Also acts as hot sausage burner, £12. Sausages sell better, will not be separated, £40. Or £45 each. I'll let you know. FRAmley 611.

DINING ROOM TABLE, 4ft circular extending to 8ft circular. 4 chairs extending to 8 chairs. Pure bahogany. £4. FRA491.

A PORTRAIT of your house in beautiful oils by renowned Austrian artist. £6. Also great idea for another one of those wars to end all wars. 2 guineas. SOUth Tyrol 958

NEW HARPOONS

HUGE BARREL of gin with a straw. No longer required. Was going to get paralytic, now going to learn the accordion instead. My mother says. 3 guineas or will accept the nearest offer. Apply FENWICK, Hodges Lodge, Codge.

MAJESTIC series of framed prints of Ramsay Macdonald in dry-dock. £14-3-6. Framley 590.

ELECTRIC FIRE with wood surround, coal effect, immaculate, although the faulty plug may have somewhat burned my house down. £2.7.6 for my one remaining posession. FRAmley 709

GRAMOPHONE RECORD-INGS. Latest dances [and] stage tunes from...

---

of perfume. Dizziness, nausea, eye-strain and overpowering smell of Turkish drains in high summer. Unwanted gift. 5/-. CODge 718.

CINEMA surplus stock. Set of David Lloyd George films. *The Llove Bug. David Lloyd George Rides Again. David Lloyd George Goes To Monte Carlo. David Lloyd George Goes To Bananas.* Offers welcome. Call MARY at the Polyhedron SOCKford 624

TINY MIRRORS, dozens of them. Come with three dead pet rabbits, 100% chance of your wife running off with my father and the remaining 5½ years of bad luck. 4/6 a bag FRAmley 061.

THE COTTON BOTTOM COTTON. Absorbs the ugliest of personal mistakes. Half a mile in one reel. 8½d WRIpple 640

LAMP BLACK Barrels of industrial quality substance of some sort. Possibly Lamp Black. Whatever that is. Offers to Stella at THE OLD RECTORY, Wripple.

ADVENTURE SHOES. Ideal for journeys to the dark continent or fashionable travels of an Egyptian nature. Size eight. Peril-resitant soles. He mounted compass. Convert solar topee at the flick of a lat Contact METTLESON & SO Ltd, Winch St, Framley

---

BRING BACK

The "Dancing 20's"

Strange though it is now to think, when you look at the genteel sights of the Molford bypass and Lobber's Mexicano Lobster Grill And Nashville Diner, but Framley was once regarded as the most sinful town in Britain!

In February 1922, local bandleader **Walton Pevesner**, stuck for a song to finish his set at The Sockford Mussel Fair, decided to pull a new number out of the hat. The *Negro Bump* was an instant sensation, starting a craze that lasted right through to the summer of that year and sold over 100,000 copies of itself in sheet music form, though listening to it now on a scratchy old 78 recording with my modern ears, I have to say it sounds a bit shit!

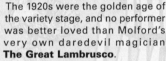

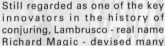

Magic Man

The 1920s were the golden age of the variety stage, and no performer was better loved than Molford's very own daredevil magician **The Great Lambrusco**.

Still regarded as one of the key innovators in the history of conjuring, Lambrusco - real name Richard Magic - devised many stage tricks that continue to be performed to this day. *Sawing Myself In Half*, *The Boring Linking Rings*, *Hiding Inside A Lion* and dozens of other classic illusions all sprang from the fertile imagination of the man they no longer called "Mr Magic".

In 1926, Lambrusco was asked to perform for His Majesty The King, the biggest show of the conjuror's life. To steady his shaky hands, Lambrusco - usually a teetotaller - downed a nerve-strengthening eighteen pints of strong cider backstage and steeled himself to perform.

Anticipation was palpable as the house lights dimmed and the curtain rose to reveal Lambrusco. Immediately the magician stunned the audience by setting off a row of fireworks reading "Goodnight", before bowing, running into the wings and attempting to hail a cab.

It was clear to his assistant that the illusionist had forgotten the running order of his show. After he was manhandled back onstage and propped against a vanishing cabinet, Lambrusco blearily stumbled through the rest of the programme with a great deal of prompting and loud reminders of which trick was which. As the finale approached with only a few errors, it seemed that victory had been snatched from the jaws of disaster.

Sadly the magician was killed moments later at the climax of the "*Ball of Doom*" finale when his assistant fired a cannonball at him from an ornamental Turkish cannon and Lambrusco attempted to saw it in half.

...ing with death, he insisted.

New Dance Craze enlivens May Day!

Fracton Fields were full to bursting with gay celebrants this May Day as hundreds of local bright young things threw caution to the wind.

They had come out to enjoy the society sounds of Walton Pevesner and His Rag Goblins, maharajahs of the new dance craze The Negro Bump! And enjoy they certainly did!

Though His Honour The Mayor had urged caution that

...later p...
by an expert in chelonian welfare.

the new fad might result in injury or, worse, encourage miscegenation and the dilution of the blood, none of the Fracton flingers seemed to care. As soon as the distinctive banjo chords rang out, the field became a mass of whirling dervishes.

Windows were flung open as soon as the first "Ouch" was heard, and the police were called. Eventually the dance had to be put down by the Royal Framley Regiment, using cannon and lance.

WAR NEWS

The battle for St Min... Mount entered its fourth... yesterday, with the loss o... lives.

The Minister For... explained that, thoug... could no longer reme... what the fight was abo... was sure the Algerians have "done something horrendous" to encourage an elongated siege.

"We are losing so many... I'm convinced this bat... probably about somethin... ribly important. Maybe... stole some land from u... were rude about the King."... f that weren't the case, h... ...n only a lunatic wou... ...in the regio...

Oh What A Lovely Great War

For all that is said about World War II a lot less is said about World War I, chiefly because most of the people alive at the time either died horribly at the time or are now horribly dead themselves.

At the same time as the Archduke of France was attacking his own head with an icepick in Mexico City, able men from all over Framley were preparing to fight the enemy armeny of Germany, armed only with the knowledge that the commanding generals would never put their lives at unnecessary risk.

In the military wing of Framley Museum, tribute is paid by the museum curators of yesterday to the fighting heroes of the day before that.

On Flanders Pitch

It was **Christmas 1917**, it was December. A football match was about to take place in a field at Ypres, later to be recognized as one of the most fiercely fought battles of the entire conflict.

"At the stroke of midnight Ernie Grebe, captain of **His Majesty's Framley Rifles First XI**, strode out into the centre of the makeshift football pitch and shook hands with his opposite number, Jürgen Wendt, Hauptmann of the 16th Baden Schleissgarten Armoured Fußball Mannschaft. The men were dripping with creamy Belgian mud and were clearly shell-shaped after the events they had both been through.

To the strains of Great British and Adequate German voices wearily chorusing traditional carols, Grebe and the Kaiser's loyal servant offered up their small firearms to each other. "Merry Christmas Fritz, old chap", offered the seventh-generation Molford butcher. "Our nations may be at war but we should surely respect the day of Our Saviour's birth. He wouldn't want us to be playing football at such a holy time as this."

With wistful sighs, the two brave midfielders both planted a bullet firmly in the opposing forehead. As their corpses slumped lifelessly to the ground, the voices of the troops joined in unison for one last time as they let out a collectively blood-curdling festive battle cry. Carnage ensued as the fifty-three remaining soldiers battled with beribboned bayonets, neatly wrapped hand grenades, and novelty crackers."

Soldier's Days - The Great War Through The Eyes of a Molford Ironmonger, Chapter XIV. by Osland Grenache

1917

Since its kick-off at the outbreak of the Great War, the soldiers of Ypres had been playing soccer for almost 2 million minutes on what Lord Kitchener had famously described as *"the most disappointing front of the conflict"*. Finally, with the score standing at 10,201 - 10,199 to the talented Framley side, a dubious offside ruling meant that the last man standing was finished off with a canister of chlorine gas by the Belgian referee, Jacques Placque (Ypres). *Match abandoned.*

As the only town in Britain to be flattened by aerial bombardment during The First World War I, Framley certainly saw its share of trouble. Nightly bombing raids on the town were orchestrated by a young Austrian German corporal named Adolf Hitler. A struggling artist, Hitler had been furious to discover that one of his best watercolours was being used without permission as a poster to attract tourists to the region. Utilising innovative silent explosives, and pulling some favours from a couple of friends in the Krupps Munition Corps, he unleashed wave after wave of devastating **Toodlepip** bombs, only ceasing the attacks when backdated royalties were finally paid to him in unmarked Reichmarks in 1935.

1918

A Hitler

G'day, Sport!

It's not all boring old chaff in the Framley Museum, there's also a special section devoted to the competitive nature of man and wombman. In this section we take a look at the contribution of the region's more sporting folk in shaping some of the world's most popular games and cricket. How's that?

Look! Here's a popular 70s sport, golfkarting. Invented by a young Sockford resident, Barry Salve, the sport was banned by the pro-golf Home Secretary after being featured on poplar television programmes Nationwide and Why Don't You...?

Tigerracing

Whoft Stadium is now almost derelict but there was a time when it echoed to the roar of the crowd or the smell of fear. **Tigerracing** dates back to pre-Roman times and they don't stop banging on about it in the Bible, apparently, but it had gone through something of a renaissance at the turn of the sentry and, by the 1930s, street races were rife, leading many to fear for the safety of the public.

Local entrepreneur **Dr Cuthbert P. Bananaboat** had made his fortune ten years earlier through some wise investments in arse ventilation, an emergent technology that went on to save thousands of grateful lives. When, in 1930, Webster Bananaboat, his only son and heir, was savaged to ouch by a 250-pound Sumatran tiger whilst spectating at an all-night backstreet tiger derby, Bananaboat vowed to put an end to the illegal gatherings and to provide a venue in which fans could enjoy the awesome spectacle in stylish executive comfort, with a wide range of Scotch eggs, fizzbombs and novelty crisps.

Dr Cuthbert's dream finally came true in **1933**, when he awoke to find himself hiding naked in the pulpit of his local church. Bail was posted just in time to allow him to oversee the very final stages of the stadium's construction. Events were then staged thrice weekly with excited locals thronging to the track, where their favourite big cats would have to chase down a live greyhound strapped to a monorail. Race distances ranged from three quarters of an inch to 18 miles if the going was soft.

The star of the track was **The Brilliant Mrs Nehru**, a stylish tigress from Mt. Himalaya. She forged a lasting partnership with her jockey - Littleted Griffiths - and became something of a celebrity in 1935 when she was the first female to win the BBC Sports Personality of the Year Award.

A devoutly religious Bananaboat initially refused to allow gambling at the stadium. However, after much pressure from his family and as a result of his death at the age of 73, he decided to relax his objections. Sadly, this proved to be the final nail in the corpse for the tigers who had always aligned themselves with their patron's strict moral code. Their 6-month work-to-rule saw them all starve to death by October 1941, and loyal fans were forced to take up new interests, such as the nascent sport of Hippodeo.

Blah blah

As part of the African land grab of the mid-Victorian era, a one-sided agreement was reached whereby division of territory would be decided by limited-over cricket matches.

In 1874 the **Galeka tribe** of the Southern African Cape Colony were challenged to a 55-over game by Prince Albert and the **Sockford Extraordinary Gentlemen.**

The clash was famously the last cricket match that Queen Victoria ever attended (a well-struck six hit her squarely on the nose, leading her to declare "We are not unhurt"). The pioneering Sockford heroes batted first and managed an innings total of 312 for 2 before blunderbussing the Africans out for no runs at all.

Before returning to Old Blighty, Her Majesty decided to colour her newly acquired bit of atlas pink (after her favourite flavour of custard) using the same felt-tip pen that she had used to colour in all the other bits of her Empire.

Oh, how she loved her custard!

bloody blah

Framley's Sporting Heroes

TUMOUR'S CIGARETTES

FRAMLEY SPORTING HEROES
A SERIES OF 12

Frank Tomorrow

Local legend Frank "The Destroyer" Tomorrow began his boxing career in the 1920s and is still considered a heavyweight title challenger by his wife. Knockout victories over Jack Dempsey and Sugar Loaf Mountain will almost certainly have earned him his eternal place in boxing heaven.

ISSUED BY
ALAN TUMOUR & SONS
A BRANCH OF THE IMPERIAL MINT & CIGARETTE CO. OF GT. BRITAIN & IREL. LTD.

TUMOUR'S CIGARETTES

FRAMLEY SPORTING HEROES
A SERIES OF 12

Vicky Kettner

Belle of the 1948 St. Moritz Winter Olympics, the glamorous ski jumper is currently thought to be orbiting somewhere around Earth. Jealous rivals waxed the slope just before her last jump, leading her to soar far above the atmosphere where she is still breaking the world record today.

ISSUED BY
ALAN TUMOUR & SONS
A BRANCH OF THE IMPERIAL MINT & CIGARETTE CO. OF GT. BRITAIN & IREL. LTD.

TUMOUR'S CIGARETTES

FRAMLEY SPORTING HEROES
A SERIES OF 12

Gregory Peg

Doyen of horse racing commentary in the 1930s. Millionaire broadcaster Peg made a fortune out of the bookmakers during the golden age of radio. The advent of television made it far more difficult to fool them however and his commentaries became slightly more accurate.

ISSUED BY
ALAN TUMOUR & SONS
A BRANCH OF THE IMPERIAL MINT & CIGARETTE CO. OF GT. BRITAIN & IREL. LTD.

TUMOUR'S CIGARETTES

FRAMLEY SPORTING HEROES
A SERIES OF 12

Diddy Fataar

Known as the golfer's caddy of choice, Ftaah fell from grace during the US Open of 1987. Ian Woosnam was disqualified in the third round when marshals discovered that a second Ian Woosnam had been packed in the bag, one more than the regulation number of Ian Woosnams allowed.

ISSUED BY
ALAN TUMOUR & SONS
A BRANCH OF THE IMPERIAL MINT & CIGARETTE CO. OF GT. BRITAIN & IREL. LTD.

FRAMLEY SPORTING HEROES
A SERIES OF 12

Stanley Lebor

Framley's first British Bulldog representative at international level. Talent scouts spotted Lebor breaking an older boy's arm in the playground, and he made the first of 57 England appearances soon after. Lebor turned pro in 1973, before retiring to become Chancellor of The Exchequer in 1986.

ISSUED BY
ALAN TUMOUR & SONS
A BRANCH OF THE IMPERIAL MINT & CIGARETTE CO. OF GT. BRITAIN & IREL. LTD.

FRAMLEY SPORTING HEROES
A SERIES OF 12

Reginald Singular

Whoft darts player who holds the record for the most repeated sporting clip on UK television. The public seemingly never tire of seeing Reg score a maximum 147 with one dart before swallowing the other two and running head first into the board, screaming "I could have been the next Larry Adler!"

ISSUED BY
ALAN TUMOUR & SONS
A BRANCH OF THE IMPERIAL MINT & CIGARETTE CO. OF GT. BRITAIN & IREL. LTD.

Framley's Sporting Heroes

TUMOUR'S CIGARETTES

FRAMLEY SPORTING HEROES
A SERIES OF 12

Drake Balustrade

The "three-minute egg" had always been thought beyond man's capability until Balustrade ran a three-minute mile on May 5, 1954 with a Primus stove strapped to his back. The soft-boiled egg was perfect and he was presented with the Order of the Dippy Soldier in the 1956 Birthday Honours.

ISSUED BY
ALAN TUMOUR & SONS
A BRANCH OF THE IMPERIAL MINT & CIGARETTE CO. OF GT. BRITAIN & IREL. LTD.

D. BALUSTRA

TUMOUR'S CIGARETTES

FRAMLEY SPORTING HEROES
A SERIES OF 12

Bill "Fats" Davies

Snooker champ Davies was the hero of the 1937 World Masters Champ--ionship in Munich. Despite Nazi assertions that Aryans were the dominant snookering race, Fats dazzled the Germans with his skill, setting back the start of WWII by 19 months while Hitler furiously practised his rest shot..

ISSUED BY
ALAN TUMOUR & SONS
A BRANCH OF THE IMPERIAL MINT & CIGARETTE CO. OF GT. BRITAIN & IREL. LTD.

"FATS" DAVIES

FRAMLEY SPORTING HEROES
A SERIES OF 12

Polly Jones–Jones

Jones-Jones made headlines at Wimbledon in 1961, the Queen's Pottery Jubilee year. Polly lifted national pride by reaching the semi-finals of the Ladies' Singles draw only to be disqualified when a locker room incident led a young Billie Jean King to raise suspicions about Polly's gender

ISSUED BY
ALAN TUMOUR & SONS
A BRANCH OF THE IMPERIAL MINT & CIGARETTE CO. OF GT. BRITAIN & IREL. LTD.

TUMOUR'S

P. JONES-JONE

TUMOUR'S CIGARETTES

M. MELTON

FRAMLEY SPORTING HEROES
A SERIES OF 12

Mowbray Melton

Sockford's swimming Olympian, Mowbray Melton competed in the 1976 and 1980 Games for Great Britain. He had the honour of carrying the flag at both opening ceremonies and perhaps would have qualified from his 100m freestyle heats if he hadn't still been holding onto it.

ISSUED BY
ALAN TUMOUR & SONS
A BRANCH OF THE IMPERIAL MINT & CIGARETTE CO. OF GT. BRITAIN & IREL. LTD.

FRAMLEY SPORTING HEROES
A SERIES OF 12

Brian St. Ilton

Five-time winner of the Tour de France, the Molford sportsman earned his victories by sitting on the handlebars of Eddy Merckx's bike during the 1960s and 1970s. The 1972 race saw the closest ever finish to the Tour with St. Ilton beating the Belgian by just .067 of a second overall.

ISSUED BY
ALAN TUMOUR & SONS
A BRANCH OF THE IMPERIAL MINT & CIGARETTE CO. OF GT. BRITAIN & IREL. LTD.

B. ST.

TUMOUR'S CIGARETTES

FRAMLEY SPORTING HEROES
A SERIES OF 12

Rusty

This Jack Russell terrier achieved notoriety when he stole and buried the World Cup trophy, on loan to the Framley Museum in the summer of 1968. Upon the return of the missing item, Rusty was encased in 24-carat gold and later presented to the Brazilian soccer team following their third victory in 1970.

ISSUED BY
ALAN TUMOUR & SONS
A BRANCH OF THE IMPERIAL MINT & CIGARETTE CO. OF GT. BRITAIN & IREL. LTD.

The Legacy of Barone

Guiglielmo Barone, inventor of the lap, is perhaps Framley's most famous son. Born in Rimini in 1875, he moved to England as a lad, and settled happily in a beautiful Gregorian town house near Denegate *(see right)*.

In 1895, Signor Barone successfully achieved the first lap under laboratory conditions, and in 1896 conducted brilliant experiments that led to the formation of the **Barone Lap Company Ltd.**

FRAMLEY BOROUGH COUNCIL

GUIGLIEMO BARONE
1874-1937
LAP PIONEER
Lived here
1918-1930

One of Barone's many early prototypes. *(Barone archive)*

In **1922**, Barone launched his breakthrough lap on the public, describing it as *"a rendering of the body so as to make sitting on horizontal surfaces possible and eradicate the need to lean awkwardly at 45 degrees to the natural world."*

On a live radio broadcast from the BBC's studios in Victoria Palace, Barone was heard to say, *"Come here, Mr Sciccicciccicicini. I'm sitting down,"* and, at a stroke, the lap was born.

Barone's pioneering invention caught on like yawning. By the mid-1920s, most households had a revolutionary *'settee,'* and had thrown out their 45° leaning boards, or *'proppies'*. Although a rise in the number of recorded back problems followed, Barone's lap was rightly recognised as a massive breakthrough.

Without the lap, now a universally acclaimed way of sitting down, we would never have had chat shows, laptop computers or cats, and Barone would no doubt have died a poor immigrant. But with it, we live in a relaxing world full of delightful sitting down.

From our armchairs all over the planet, we salute you, Guiglielmo Barone!

1926 Up Up!

The hard financial times of the inter-war years saw people all over the world looking for ways of forgetting their troubles. Whether it was laughing at silent comedians like Jeff and Other Jeff, wheeling with gay abandon at a maths marathon, or simply jumping from a fifteenth storey Wall Street window to your death, everyone was on the look-out for new thrills.

Sockford Aerodrome in 1926 was the venue for a short-lived craze that combined this taste for edge-of-the-seat entertainment with two other contemporary obsessions - aviation and bar billiards.

The daredevil acts of the **Bellaire Billiard Barnstormers** made front page news and packed out the Sockford airfield to the extent that scarecrows had to be erected to keep spectators off the runways.

The craze produced tie-in toys and games, but was banned in 1927 when an onlooker was struck and killed by a plummetting mushroom, scoring 150 points.

And Away!

Fancy a Nice Brewer?

Of all our local industries, there is one above all others that should be prepared to take responsibility for the decline of industry in the area. Stand up and take a bow, **Puddles of Whotten Plodney**, we salute your beer and the marvellous number of sick days that it causes!.

Established around the time of King Nelson I, Puddles was set up by a collective of serious drinkers, all of whom had been banned from every hostelry in the area after leading the notorious Whit Sunday Riot of 1808 - 1811.

Today the brewery produces **82** varieties of beer, **33** of which are legal and **6** of which are palatable. In fact I'm actually enjoying **1** as I write this - a foaming pint of *Luftwaffe Bitte*. It really is highly addictive and sometimes, on the darkest nights, I think it might be my only friend.

* **Pictures courtesy Puddles Brewery Inc.)**

As early as the 1932s, posters for Puddles were sticking themselves up all over the county.

Featuring the alarmingly strict character, **Barroclough the Serpent**, the adverts adopted a sermonising tone on original sin. After scaring away more customers than the company actually had, the serpent character was replaced by the friendlier **Barroclough the Snake**.

Instead of preaching at drinkers, Barroclough now swallowed them whole, giving us the phrase *"down in one".*

A reproduction of a 1959 campaign poster, as voiced by Bernard Cribbins.

The reptile motif was finally replaced in the mid-1960s, when Bernard Cribbins donated his voice to a series of television commercials with the slogan *"Just what the doctor ordered you not to drink".*

Advertising the booze

Did you know... ...

that a cartoon sketch on an early Puddles poster eventually developed into that ruddy-faced, bearded Christmas-time character that we all know so well - the Pissed-Up Uncle?

The Booze

Some of the beers and the ciders and the stouts and the pale ales that have rightly made Puddles of Whotten Plodney a success story to rival any of the success stories that I've ever heard of.

 Luftwaffe Bitte - light bitter, 3.8% ABV - *Night out in Coventry*

 Methodman - premium cask bitter 4.279% ABV - *There's a little moustachioed clog dancer trapped inside my head*

 Old Laxative - strong bitter, 5% ABV *Goes in slow, comes out fast*

 Mind Meld - cider, 30% HGV - *Sharper than a steak-knife sandwich*

 Wripple St George - stout, 30 MPH - *As if being swallowed by a snake*

 Wripple's Drink It Or Not - not too sure, 1964 - *Crunchy, Russ Conway playing in the corner*

 Reality Check - india pail ail, 100% ABV - *Where's your head at? No, really, where's your head gone?*

Why not visit the Puddles of Whotten Plodney exhibit, located on one of the floors somewhere in the Framley Museum?

Well, here are some of the reasons to (do that) that you can read now.

Mums and/or dads can leave the kids to wander around the museum in the company of one of our trained childhandlers and enjoy a soothing pint or pints.

Dress up as a pint glass with a foam hat and refractive dimples.

The entire 1976 Formula One season on a continuous loop in the saloon bar section.

Shirts must be worn, no football colours.

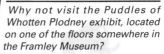

REMEMBER: Don't drink too much and drive!

The Historic Pubs of Framley

The town of Framley was limited to a maximum number of 49 pubs by Royal Decree after the 1836 census revealed that every single building in the town centre was a pub. Special dispensation was given in 1974 for a 50th pub to open, the Hawaii 5-0, on the corner of Going For Gold Avenue and Denegate. On these pages, we visit all fifty of them and point out some points of historical interest for the casual drunk.

The Cock *(High St)* 18th Century coaching inn. Edwardian Scotch Egg machine in Gents.

The Balls *(Well Lane)* Disabled toilets (no flush).

The Berk *(Storming Glade)* Original Victorian seating, lamps, *Mind Your Language* fruit machine.

The Queen's Furniture *(Harbour Walk)* Public, saloon & hatchback bars.

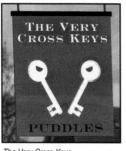

The Very Cross Keys

The Very Cross Keys *(Sallyfields)* Site of the infamous 1960s gangland murder of Jack 'The Body' Hurley, a victim of the notorious Brother Twins. The villains filled Jack's hat full of lead, killing him by a combination of lead poisoning and a sore neck. Visitors can still see the original swagger marks on the door frame from when the twins used to enter the bar.

The Duke of Everywhere *(Daddio Square)* The cloth landlord dates from the early Georgian period.

The Inn on the Move *(Phone for details)* Credit will only be given to those patrons over 70 if accompanied by both grandparents!

The Swan *(Dennis Waterman Lane)* Unlicensed. Bring your own booze.

The Swan *(Octopus Street)* Bisto dispenser on bar.

Here Be Turnips *(Gentlemen Rise)* The first pub in the area. People gathered on the site around 1130 drawn by the promise of a sign in the ground, and stood around waiting to see the turnips. A pub developed naturally. Original Victorian doors.

The Swan *(Galleon's Reach)* Occasionally underwater. Amazing riverbed views.

The Swan *(The All-New Adventures of Bruce Foxton Avenue)* Penicillin was first used here.

The Original Swan *(Biro Street)* Famously open in 1933 by Laurel & Hardy. Closed later that ye when Stan got trapped in a barrel and Ollie w arrested by James Finlayson dressed as policeman. Under new management.

The Swan *(Bungo Avenue)* Beautiful 1930s Toile decorated in Scrabble tiles. Fans will be glad to nd that "Now wash your hands" is on a triple wo score.

The Swan *(Mouth Street)* Contains the 16 Century bannister that Mary, Queen of Poppi famously slid up to her doom.

The New Swan *(Q-Bert Avenue)* Patrons inclu Ian Fleming, creator of Sir Sean Connery and t Grape Gonzo.

The Running Mayor *(The Hollies)* The inn sign commemorates an important annual event in Framley's history.

The Wednesday Play *(Round Square)* Built from wood taken from the pub next door (see *The Pub That Collapsed*, Chatto & Windbag, 1968).

The Running Ma

The Public House of the Rising Sun *(Dar Corner)* Framley's hottest pub since records bega

Molly Quickly's Gin Hospital *(Pork Wa* Rumoured to be the inspiration for the pub *Chee* from TV's *The Frasier Crane Show*.

My Other Pub is a Hotel *(Marmite Place)* T carpark was the site of an historic duel in 18 between the great-grandfathers of Paul Simon & Garfunkel.

The Burnt Lunch *(Chevron Chase)* HRH Prin Andrew, Duke of York was conceived here round t back by the bins.

he Jolly Pocket Postman *(Rosie's Walk)* The eautiful antique Colour Separation Overlay wall atures views of whatever you want and was used as e location for the 1962 film of *Lawrence of Arabia*.

he Ploughman's Lump *(Pleasant Crescent)* An dwardian gantry drops asses onto the heads f customers, saving atrons the trouble of arting fights themselves.

e Crunch Bunch *Duracell Wall)* Home of e Miami Dolphins.

ainsbury's *Taste he Difference* Pub *Belgian Tramp Avenue)* FK was shot here.

The Ploughman's lump

he Frightful Boar *(La La Lane)* Patrons can see a eautifully maintained Victorian argument about the rimean War still going on in the corner of the snug.

he Debtor's Oblivion *(Chauncey Gardens)* esigned and built in eleven minutes by renowned Sth Century liar Jereboam Fowlkes. *"The only pub Framley."*

he Bernie Inn *(Braces Court)* Unspoilt since 1986.

he Pelican't *(Bristow Mansions)* Antique pine oak beer garden.

he Tale of Jemima Puddlepub *(Tilbrook Glen)* hat's me in the corner. Hello!

he St Greavesie *(The Fry's Five Centre)* A nnel linking this pub to an old Ford Capri parked in e Arnhem Centre was used by smugglers in the Sth Century to hide the looted husks of pirates.

he Hottentot & Blowdart *(Colonial Alley)* Framley's ird oldest pub. "Exotic" decor may offend.

he Beer *(Pam Ferris Terrace)* In 1911, a gang of ystery-solving kids spent a night in the old wine cellar oping to catch a glimpse of the resident ghost. Sure ough, at the stroke of midnight, they were drunk.

he Commoner's Muck *(Polyfilla Villas)* On the all hang portraits of the current clientele. Please ook well in advance and send a passport-sized hotograph at least 48 hours before your visit.

he Shy Crabs *(Roadway Close Street Gardens)* andlord missing since 1967.

he Simon Horse & Simon Groom *(Unseemly arade)* The public bar features an unusually wide ahogany barmaid.

The Where Was I Meant To Be Going *(Venison Haunch Drive)* Beautifully preserved 14th century regulars.

The Pressgang & Prostitute *(Big Court)* Original 19th Century Captain's Table with varnished fish fingers.

The Drinker's Untimely End *(Nilsson Point)* Contains five more pubs in beer garden by appointment to HRH Princess Margaret.

O'Crikey's *(Spiller's Mr Dog Road)* No beer.

The Double or Drop *(Unit P74, Dullfields Ind Est)* Famous patrons include George Best and our Lord & Saviour Our Lord Jesus Christ.

The Burke & Hare & Hounds *(Different Heights)* You don't have to be mad to drink here but it helps that the staff have been certified as clinically insane. Brilliant floors.

The Stop! Hammer Time *(Grenade Parade)* A nautical theme inside, with pictures of naval scenes and the top half of an 18th Century sailor protruding from the toilet cistern. Some risk of scurvy.

You Can't Touch This

The Real Queen Victoria *(Pornmead)* The long-standing alcohol ban imposed by Prince Albert after his fat wife died makes it impossible to get a drink other than tomato juice or landlord's nightwater. A waste of your time, my time, and valuable real estate.

Club FoXXXy *(Magic Roundabout)* This fourteenth century coaching inn was refurbished beautifully in 1986 in the Athena style, with Garfield pint glasses and wax heads of Don Johnson.

The Viscount of Orange *(Lunchbox Crescent)* The original landlord is commemorated by an angrily lifelike Victorian automaton who turfs out recalcitrant drinkers at 8.45pm sharp, dipping their wallets before pissing oil down its front.

The Richard Scarry's Biggest Busiest Pub Ever *(Lowly Worm Street)* Chef Farmer Alfalfa cooks Thai food for a lively cardboard animal crowd.

The Prospect of Going Home Drunk *(The Shits)* A variety of Edwardian boardgames are on offer, all covered in dog slobber.

Hawaii 5-0 *(Keystone Copse)* See below.

A Brush with History

To art lovers, the sleepy villages around Sockford have a special name - *Bethsheveth Country* - for it is and was here that **Ibrahim Bethsheveth**, the grand old man of Framley painting worked and works.

Bethsheveth was born in Sockford in 1909, but had to wait until 1931 before his first major exhibition, at the **Keysel Gallery** in Molford. Centred on the female nude, and painted in his soon-to-be-trademark frenzied, one-handed style, Bethsheveth's paintings made him an overnight sensation.

The critics were unanimous - here was a bright new talent. Elizabeth Macaque of the *Whoft Sentinel* made particular mention of the way that, no matter where she stood in the gallery, the artist seemed to follow her round the room.

1936 is generally agreed to be the zenith of Bethsheveth's golden period, with works such as *Nude Descending A Staircase Viewed Through Frosted Glass And Binoculars* and *Nude Hiding Herself With A Bedsheet Whilst Nude Man With Moustache Levels Shotgun At Artist* representing the peak of his artistic achievement.

As his reputation grew, so did the price tags on his paintings. Eventually the tags became sought-after collectors items themselves - a sale of gallery labels from the artist's 1932-1936 period broke auction house records in 1947 - which just goes to show.

Bethsheveth in 1931, shortly before the exhibition that made his reputation.

Design of the times

Always keen to stretch himself, and subject to a restraining order that kept him from his customary subjects on pain of imprisonment, Bethsheveth accepted a government post in 1951, working in the design department of the Ministry of Britain.

It was here that he created one of post-war Britain's least-loved characters, **Onion Jack**. The almost endearing onion-headed bulldog mascot was intended to keep spirits high in the austere years following the Brilliant War. As it turned out, Jack served as *"The Nation's Friend"* for less than six months of unprecedented public indifference before being replaced by the successful "Toby The Jug" character who can still be seen on stamps and coins - and the £25 note - to this day.

Bethsheveth didn't take the perceived failure of his creation lying down, and continued to offer the little dog to other companies and institutions. For three ghastly months, brass Onion Jack badges were given away with jars of Empire Marmalade, before protests from just about everybody forced the company to revert to their usual caricatures of gypsies.

The stubborn artist even designed the logo and programme for the 1958 **Framley World's Fair** for free in return for permission to erect a spectacular Onion Jack pavilion on the riverside walk. Tragically the weight of the first two visitors to Bethsheveth's masterpiece caused the spherical head section of the pavilion to become detached from its plexiglass body and tumble into the river, drowning the policemen instantly.

A china model of an illustration of a china model of the unloved character (1954).

Time Flies By When You're Doing Your Page In The Book

Living in Molford in the 1930s was not at all like living in Molford in the 1990s. People actually spoke to one another and a genuine sense of community was fostered.

Here we retell a story from those innocent days, assembled painstakingly by me from eyewitness reports in the Framley Museum Archive.

...was a beautiful summer's day, like ...ery day used to be in Molford, and a ...rge was chugging along the canal ...tween banks of green willow. The ...rgee could hear the distant chiming ...a town clock and before long he had ...ived at the wharf where he was to ...liver two large boxes for the town ...ll and one crate of valuable antique ...oks for Lord Bellbottom of nearby ...nkstead Hall.

Operating the cargo crane on that day was the wharfinger, a Mr Twenty-Pence. Little had he known when he awoke that morning that this would be the most exciting day of his life!

After telephoning Bellbottom's butler Hinge to inform him that the books had arrived, Mr Twenty-Pence set about lifting the crate ashore.

Splash! Oh my! The precious delivery had fallen from the crane's lifting hook before it had reached safety.

His Lordship and Hinge arrived on the footplate of their carefully restored steam speedboat just in time to see the box tumble into the canal. The books were probably ruined and the crane was a busted flush.

...thout stopping for breath, the ...arfinger called out Mr Tubbs the ...hicle recovery man and also the ...ldier boys of Cox's Fort, who ...tunately for this story had trained ...gmen amongst their ranks. Their ...ober-clad privates were able to ...ach the hook of the recovery vehicle ...the crate and it was hauled to the ...nk.

But there was a surprise for everyone when the package was opened - it wasn't the books at all! It was just lots of human livers in ice.

The bargee had been distracted when sending the delivery ashore and had attached the wrong one so Lord Bellbottom's signed first editions of *Ljubliana Slumber Party* were safe after all.

Everyone present breathed a sigh of relief and they decided to go to the local biscuit factory where a dance was held every weekday evening after the 6 o'clock whistle was blown. There they danced until morning in Bacchanalian revelry to the sound of a well-preserved, shiny Dutch organ denoting the end of another adventure for the exceedingly animated people of Molford.

More stories from historic Molford can be seen on BBC2 every lunchtime, and on a video I nicked from 4-Play in the Arnhem Centre.

CLINTON AND BEYOND

Whether it's a lungful of sea air or a face covered in clams you're after, come to Clinton! And Beyond!
The new Municipolitan Railway links Framley to the beach, the promenade, the pier, and right out to the middle of the sea, in less than 45 minutes. Come on, take the plunge!

FRAMLEY RAILWAYS

TRAVEL BY TRAIN TO THE SEA

1936

The advent of the Municipolitan Railway made quick and easy rail travel to the coast - a luxury which had previously been the preserve of royal and train drivers - a real possibility for ordinary people. Soon beautiful, balmy Clinton was full of slack-jawed oafs eating fish and chips with th
fingers, bringing in valuable revenue for the town and dropping their bloody burger wrappers in my garden.

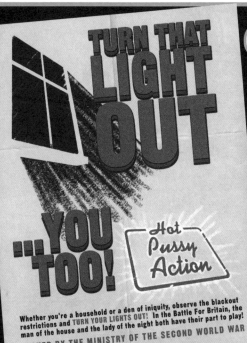

TURN THAT LIGHT OUT ...YOU TOO!

Hot Pussy Action

Whether you're a household or a den of iniquity, observe the blackout restrictions and TURN YOUR LIGHTS OUT! In the Battle For Britain, the man of the house and the lady of the night both have their part to play!

ISSUED BY THE MINISTRY OF THE SECOND WORLD WAR

1943

By 1943, German air raids were a nightly occurence in the nightly skies over Framley, and it was up to the average person in the street to observe blackout regulations and thus make it more difficult for the bomber pilots to blow everybody up than it would otherwise have been without the efforts of those ordinary people.

Posters like this one would have been a vital part of that effort. When the air raid sirens rang, everybody would run into their homes and turn all the lights off. Then they would try and hide, as quietly as possible, from the bombs. If, after the German pilots had counted to 100, no-one had been found, the Luftwaffe would return to their bases and have to do a forfeit such as kissing a girl, or eating an apple without using their mouth.

1942

War was a time of bluff and double bluff in the morale industries, with propaganda and counter-propaganda fighting it out for the hearts and minds of the people. This poster, produced by D-Section, the black propaganda unit of Framley's Communications Department shows just how elaborate the persuaders' mind games could become.

Originally commissioned to be dropped over Germany's industrial heartlands, the poster went through six separate designs, each adding an extra morale-boosting or morale-hindering element until eventually British Intelligence were convinced it was impossible to not be affected by the image, though exactly how remained unclear.

In the winter of 1942, 10,000 copies of the poster were dropped from planes over Dusseldorff, and 20,000 over Wolverhampton just to make sure. Military historians believe that posters such as this either shortened or lengthened the war by up to three years.

Don't forget that walls have cigars!

CARELESS TALK COSTS LIVES

Military Framley: RAF Harmonium

All the nice girls love a sailor, and nowhere more than around Framley. The town's association with nearby RAF Harmonium stretches back **nearly** 50 years.

The base, which is in fact a small self-contained and self-obsessed **town**, is home to more than 2,000 defence staff **and** a supply team of 650 civilianised workers.

RAF Harmonium was built in **1937** as a tactical air transport base. To raise extra funds, it doubled as a **tactful air transport base** at the weekends, when pairs of bombers flew curtains across any cloud that looked rude, which many **do**.

The village of Harmonium was largely unaffected by the **First World War**, except that all its menfolk either volunteered or were **made to volunteer** for service in the forces, and none of them came back.

The camp first opened in the 1930s, intended as a naturist colony. The airfield was originally **grass**, although it was later **glass** and, after two fatal accidents, **gladly concrete**.

Sir Malcolm Plums

Aeroplanes

RAF Harmonium opened as Number 33 Maintenance Unit in **October 1940**. On the first day, the **record book** records, there were **two** officers (Maj Gen George Bullwort and Sgt 'Alice' Johnson) and **one** civilian (the enchanting Miss Ravish).

At that time there were nine vehicles at the base - one staff car, **two wheelbarrows**, a pair of skates, an Edwardian bathing-cabinet, a **fire** engine, an ostrich and a tea-tray (for snowy conditions).

Over **the next few months**, the unit expanded, and two **runways** were built, 'Little Boy,' a 3,950ft hard runway and 'Big Chap,' a circular spongy runway for a **revolutionary** new plane that was never invented.

The station was taken over by the USAF in 1950, but their reign came to a **bloody end four** years later, when they were strung up from poles by revelling partygoers.

RAF Harmonium, home to almost 7,000 military personnel, has "both a unison and an octave coupler, and a particularly impressive 4' Bourdon stop," according to this book I've got here

Strategic Air Command based B-69 and B-MINE bombers at Harmonium, before the Station was expanded to become a tanker **and** transport base, before further expanding and expanding again during the Second Cold War.

Currently based at RAF Harmonium are the 10 VC10s of **11 Squadron**, the 11 VC11s of **10 Squadron**, the 4 VC4 C4 and 4Cs of **VC44 Squadron C**, and the 40 Forte 14-40s of the **14th Fortineers**.

Also based at RAF Harmonium is No 73 Parachute Stunt School, which includes the RAF **Synchronised Falling** Team, famous worldwide for their award-winning Sky Juggling routine.

39 Jazz Squadron doing their popular 12-bar drill.

Military Framley: War and Peace

1982

In July 1982, the Ministry of Defence tested a new weapon in the Gloveswold hills, a huge poisonous gas cloud in the shape of an **angry bear**.

Bombers from nearby RAF Harmonium dropped several ton(ne)s of the banned substance, Fortine (codenamed '14'), into the unspoilt valleys by mistake. They were supposed to be testing a new parachute disguised as a giant ladybird.

Wripple was evacuated a day later, after the vast growling cloud of **bear-shaped fury** showed more staying power than scientists had predicted, and the whole area was quarantined for three weeks.

Military police in spaceman outfits went in and sniffed out any last remaining bits of cloud **bear** with balloon-mounted hoovers, while locals were temporarily housed in primary schools, swimming pools and the boiler rooms of the town hall.

One of the Gloveswold Common women cooks lentil chops for her feral children.

Because of the incident, Gloveswold became a colourful rallying point for the anti-military lobby over the next decade, with groups of hairy women camping round the perimeter fence eating grey casserole and breast-feeding one another openly like animals.

1917

This 1917 poster was part of a drive to encourage all able-bodied men in Framley to pretend to be mental to avoid military service.

Acting Mayor **Verlaine Panda**, who devised the scheme, had himself avoided conscription quite effectively by pretending to be mad, and saw the policy as an efficient way to keep the town running smoothly. Panda was having trouble sleeping, concerned that someone might unexpectedly send his valet to the front overnight, before he'd had a chance to arrange the mayor's shoes in the right order.

At the time, Framley was operating on a skeleton staff of able-bodied men, and the Mayor was prepared to do anything to keep his last few citizens from being sent to certain death. *"If we don't act fast, I predict that within three months there won't be anybody left in the town except me. Who'll empty the bins, then?"* he memorably asked. *"Women?"*

"YOUR COUNTRY NEEDS **YOU** TO TAKE SUGAR"

1944

These bike sheds are all that remains of **Stalag Whoft 17**, the prison camp which housed the region's German prisoners of war between 1942 and '45.

The camp was disgraced in February 1944 when twenty-eight prisoners from the Baden Schleissgarten XIVth Annoying Fusiliers escaped by disguising themselves as British passports and tunnelling over the fence.

FRAMLEY at WAR

Our Finest Our

Historians would be hard pressed to argue with my belief that Britain is at its finest when it's being knocked about by bullet-headed Huns and none of us have anything to eat except rubble. When **World War II** came to Framley in 1941, with the compromise of the Framley-Schleissgarten Non Aggression Pact, the hardy townspeople were ready, and we've never enjoyed ourselves so much!

MOLFORD PICTORIAL Oct 14, 1943

Molford Pictorial

SO GRATEFU

OUR PLUCKY LADS

"**T**HREE CHEERS FOR THE GIRLS BACK HOME; - Hip, Hip! - Hooray! - Hip, Hip! - Hooray! HIP!! - HOO-RAY!!" went the soldiers.

These plucky lads are relaxing between periods of fighting the dreadful enemy in Africa. Shown, from left, are John Fault, Leonard Bleedesley, Mortimer Snif, Reggie Picklecot, William Wallopson, Derry 'The Dentist' Minuet, Fantismium Louche-Legate and Robin, the simple one.

Picklecot, 32, from Swansea, admitted that while most of the war was "a cross between a party and a series of explosions," he was missing his mother's cooking.

"I can't wait to get back to some rare Dutch Welshbit," he admitted, "the powdered stuff just isn't the same."

Wallopson, 23, from Framley, said his mother's cooking was like "the bad bits left over when you do shoes," but confessed to a trifling homesickness.

"I miss the missus, the locals and the fluff," he said.

Bleedesley, 37, from the Isle of Size, sent his regards to *Pictorial* readers, and told them "not to worry - the boys are never short of a pint of refreshing gravy," as shown in our photograph.

Robin waved and spat.

1943

BISMARCK BOBS BACK TO SURFACE

OBSERVERS reported on Tuesday that the German flagship *The Bismarck* has bobbed annoyingly back to the surface, as if challenging Allied naval forces to sink it agai

1942

In early 1942, the Framley Fluff Mills turned themselves over full-time to army supply manufacture to help the war effort, which meant a whole new form of wartime hardship for the men of the town.

Beard rationing was strictly enforced in Framley from April 1942, requiring that all facial hair be requisitioned and turned into heavy greatcoats to use as summe kit for soldiers at El Alamein (due to the same clerical error, the following winter was spent making flip-flops for Russian troops at Stalingrad).

The scheme was initially unpopular but soon the men of Framley adapted with characteristic British resourcefulness, sprucing themselves up for a night on the town by smearing gravy browning over their chins, and drawing rakish moustaches on their upper lips using eyebrow pencils.

WAAFI girls enjoy their boyfriends' bear

Within a year, the Beard Warden was a common enough sight to b immortalised on radio via character such as Warden Morden in *The Gaiet Gang*, walking the streets collectin shavings in his helmet and shatterin the morning calm with his hearty cry o "Get That Beard Off!"

WESTON *Biscuit*

MADE BY THE LARGEST BISCUIT MAKERS IN THE EMPIRE

BBC *wireless*

NOV 1944

MOST REQUESTED Gramophone Recordings

1. ' HANG OUT THE WASHING ON THE CIRCLE LINE '
.... *Dame Jeff Lynn*

2. ' IN THE NUDE '
.... *Naughty Glenn Miller & His Naughty Orchestra*

3. ' CARELESS TALK COSTS LIVES '
.... *The Ministry Of Information*

4. ' SOLDIERS MAKE MARVELLOUS HUSBANDS '
.... *Bing Crosby & The Belles Of St Wolfgang*

5. ' BULLY BEEF '
.... *Billy Balls*

6. ' THE NICE BITS OF DOVER '
.... *Gracie Cloth*

7. ' IT'S A LONGER WAY TO LONDON '
.... *The Tipperary Sisters*

8. ' INNA LAND-A DUB '
.... *The Cyril Sammes Society Choir*

9. ' SING SOMETHING ELSE '
.... *The Cliff Adams Jingles*

10. ' I DANCED (ON HITLER'S MOUSTACHE) '
.... *'Crazy' Henry Volume & Stereo Boyd*

11. ' FIZZBOMB FOXTROT '
.... *The Bee Gees*

12. ' LES GOUPILES DANS SON CUIR CHEVELU '
.... *Thierry Ballooone*

13. ' RUBBISH! RUBBISH! '
.... *Sid Flannels & The Rubbish Seven*

14. ' FILIGREE '
.... *Pontette*

15. ' IT'S YOPPING WITH RAIN '
.... *The Trolleybus Slatterns*

44

or many Framley residents, a stirring song on the wireless
as just the tonic to help forget that we were all going to die.

1942

If you lived through the dark days of the war, you're sure to remember the gay yellow livery of the Ministry of Information's **Morse Code delivery vans.**

Framley was the only district to adopt the MCDV scheme, intended to confound enemy attempts to ascertain the size of the Allied armies. Each van was decorated with a bold red dot or dash, visible from up to 500 yards away. In the event of any soldier being declared Missing In Action, a fleet of government vans would arrive at the home of his widow, alerting her with a jaunty parp on the horn. The vans would then drive past in strict order, the pattern of their dots and dashes informing her of the situation in Morse Code.

This system was, according to the Ministry, *"almost impervious"* to interception or distortion, and *"a more efficient use of fuel, hardware and manpower than the costly process of training an operative to use an expensive telegraph machine."*

In 1968, a survey by Framley Council revealed that over a hundred and twenty Framley widows who were out at the time the vans drove past, or simply unfamiliar with Morse Code, were still waiting for their husbands to return. Thankfully a more modern scheme devised by the Public Records Office, involving singing telegrams and stunt skywriting allowed the grieving parties to be brought up to speed.

FRAMLEY at WAR

1944

To free up factories to produce things the country really needed, like Spitfires and Dolly Mixtures, rationing was introduced. Every citizen was given a **ration book** which allowed them a certain, limited quantity of selected staple items, such as food, while offering loads and loads of all the other rubbish the government had found lying about in warehouses that would be better put to use as aeroplane hangars.

Rationing was abandoned in Framley in 1955, and in St Eyots in 1992, except for bacon and anal sex.

MINISTRY OF EATING

RATION BOOK

HOLDER'S NAME AND REGISTERED

Compare these details with the name sewn into your shirt. Report any discrepancies to a policeman.

DO NOT ALTER

Surname *Wilson*

Other Names *Kingtut*

Address *43 Woolis Avenue, Topney St Oh'*

ISSUED JULY 1944

NAT. REG. No. *BNCP 215 6*

If found, return to:

FOOD OFFICE

DEPT of MALNUTRITION

SERIAL NUMBER OF BOOK

PG 554 09

Do NOT attempt to eat this book

1944

elected

Betty Service says

Spring-clean your face

Your Face Puff

How often do you wash your face puff? If it's more seldom than daily, you're heading for a dirty and disgusting future. Your face will erupt in weals and chancres, and seizures will reduce you to a rictus of lop-sidedness. You will also go bald and smell.

Your Elbow Cream

Jars get dirty and smutty at the rim, and whiffy and squiffy at the lid. Wash the cream out of it completely and disinfect it every half a fortnight. Use no less than one jar of cream per elbow per ablution. Failure to follow these rules will result in Arthritic Spasm, or, worse still, Bizarre Arm.

Your Tooth Net

If you smooth your eyebrows with brilliantine or scintilline, you may find they collect dust, and, in some cases, become nests for filthy little creatures. Remove your eyebrows by sucking and eat them. Disinfect their remains with Vizmo or Biff, and draw on new eyebrows with a brow tip pencil. It's safer and looks worse.

Your Suspenders

You'll find they don't wear too well after a thorough wash. If you detect difficulties in dipping your girdle, blow it with hot salt and see how much dirt falls off. Remove it at the first sign of firmness, and your girdle will look as good as you.

Inside Your Hairbrush

Make sure you wash your hairbrush following every shampoo or egg white. Millions upon million of bacteriaes can make it their home, including the deadly **oculis avis digites pisces**, or Follicle Pigeon. Use water and lye flakes in a blend of caustic and Blanc-o.

The Intimates

Don't forget not to forget your intimates. Armpits should be regularly shaved with a tomato knife, undercarriage treated with essence of lime and merkin bitters. The Unspeakables can be douched, and The Unbelievable can be worried with the nice end of a peacock furniture duster.

Whether was brushin shrapnel o of your sca or finding the rig camouflage cream match Autum colouring, the war mu have been dreadful f personal groomin I expect. I don't knov I was only born in 197

Judging by thi clipping though, the were plenty of wome in need of advice, an this clipping shows th very clearly. (LEFT)

> TAG < get one of the girls to do this

RATION COUNTERFOIL PAGE 5

Name _Knight Wilson_ (BLOCK LETTERS)

Signature or signature tune _____

Address _43 Woolis Avenue_ (BLOCK LETTERS) Date _1st Aug 1944_

Name and Address of Retailer _Jensen's The Redcast Main Street Whott_

BD **544786**

PAGE 5

Name (BLOCK LETTERS) _Knight Wilson_

Address (BLOCK LETTERS) _43 Woolis Avenue Gopnes St Oh_

1 PUDDLE OF LEMONADE	**6** LBS OF CHALK	**1** GAME OF FOOTBALL
1 A DECKCHAIR FULL OF SPRING ONIONS	**1** FLUSH OF YOUR TOILET	**1/3** OF A PARACHUTE
8 STICKS OF ROCK	**1** ENORMOUS GORGONZOLA	**3** MATCHING SHOES	**2/3** OF AN O.B.E.	**4** CLOTHES
2/6 OF A GILL OF "HAIR QUINC"	**2** CHILDHOOD MEMORIES	**1** PLAYING CARD	DUMFRIES AND GALLOWAY	**1** BOXING GLOVE
1 PEREGRINE FALCON	**TRIPLE WORD SCORE**	**2** SAND CASTLES	**1** RATION BOOK	**1** PRINCESS BUTTERFLY'S HAND IN MARRIAGE
4 OPINIONS ON THE FRENCH	**3** WATER	**1** CRY OF RELIEF ("HURRAH!")	**48** GALLONS OF COOKING SHERRY	**1/2** A PINCH OF SALT

1943

Despite the gloom, it wasn't all gloom! One of the fun memories many have of Framley's wartime days is the cheeky secret code used to send messages between lovers separated by the conflict.

Regardless of the best efforts of army censors, a simple scrawled message on the back of an envelope could convey a world of saucy meaning. Some of the favourites include:

N.O.R.F.O.L.K.

KNICKERS OFF READY FOR OTHER LACY KNICKERS

F.R.A.M.L.E.Y.

FONDLY REMEMBERED ANNIVERSARY MATTERS LESS EACH YEAR

W.H.O.F.T.

WE'RE HAVING OTTER FOR TEA

S.W.A.N.K.

SECRET WANK

I.P.U.S.U.W.O.S.L.A.C.S.D.

I'VE PICKED UP SOMETHING UNPLEASANT WHILST ON SHORE LEAVE AND CAN'T SIT DOWN

St Eyot's Flugel

No. 1,647 — Oct. 11 1945 — Twopence

BICYCLE IS IN A TREE

"WELL, THAT'S THE LAST THING I expected to see when I was coming back,"

So exclaimed WCmdr Peter 'Picketty' Witch as he surveyed his garden last week.

Poor old Picketty's got his bicycle stuck inside a tree.

"I must have left it stood over the shoot of a sapling," he continued, "and when I come back from five long years fighting the Bosch, here it is grown around it into a fully-fledged adult tree of the like."

Although it sounds like the work of the impossible, local arboriculturist Sedney Pincloon comes to the same conclusion.

"I've witnessed this going-on before, saw a willow grow around a football. Remarkable what Mother Nature can swallow, isn't it?"

WCmdr Witch is now considering donating his tree-bicycle bicycle-tree to the St Eyot's Museum. He says he will turn the profit to buying a new bike and getting "a right beating."

1945

St Eyot's Museum donated the tree / bike / bike / tree to Framley Museum in 1971, after a ten-year old boy died trying to do a wheelie on it. It has been locked away ever since.

MASSAGE & TURKISH FOOTBALL

VERY PETTY GIRL OFFER SENSY MASSAGE AND IMPERSONATION OF TURKISH FOOTBALLERS

COST BY THE HOUR

清 英 **CENTER PLACE HOTEL, YMPAN** 恩

ROOM CHARGED EXT...

BEER VALUE!!

CLUB **Crab** 和

平 神

Kissy Kissy Teeny Weeny Yellow Polka Dot Y-Fronts

TROPHIES FROM THE FAR EAST. ▲
Military historians will be excited to learn that Framley Museum is home to the Barham Bequest which occupies most of the third floor.

THE MOLFORD & DISTRICT MESS
Classified Advertisi

* * * * * * * * * *
BUY & SELL
* * * * * * * * * *

ENORMOUS silk stockings made from entire parachute. Also tiny, useless parachute made from single pair of silk stockings. £1. FRA5789, after 6pm.

DOG BRYLCREEM. Tidy unsightly mutt hair into slick styles. Streamlines airedales for action. Transforms untidy sheepdog into shiny black sphere. As used by Dennis Compton's dachshund "Wickets". 2/- a box. FRA6454.

BANANA. £1/2m ono. Contact Vince on FRA6323.

ASSORTED RUBBLE. Bricks. Window frames. Doors. Wireless sets. Money. Hats. The top third of a barrage balloon. All guaranteed looted with certificate of authenticity. Offers. Call Malcolm on FRA6922.

WAR SECRETS. Invasion plans. Rolls of careless talk in 30, 40 and 50 yard lengths. Plenty available from our warehouse. Contact Haw Haw and Sons Ltd. FRA7471

BOTTOMLESS PIT bull terriers. Guaranteed no mess. 3/6 each. WHOft 9904

LOST : Horizon. My world now has no vanishing point and things hundreds of miles away block my vision. Call tiny Helen on an enormous telephone in the distance. FRA1749.

PATHÉ NEWSREEL footage of the coronation of King Majesty The Queen in 5 cans. God save the Quing! £1. Framley 8345

I.C.E. system for Tiger tank. Subwoofer, turret-mounted bass bins, 36mm anti-theft system. £1. SOC6630

to the name of "Dr Graham Moulding". May be scared and confused. Please call Mrs Moulding on FRAmley 0522.

HOME WANTED for evacuee. Preferably near / on Dresden, the Ruhr Dam or Nagasaki. Reasonable prices paid. Call Dr E.G. Hollyhock on Fram 6765

PAMPHLET. "The Truth About Digging For Victory - The Tunnels YOU Built". The folded sheet of paper they wanted to ban! 1/-. CliNton 831

* * * * * * * * * *
ONION SURPLUS
* * * * * * * * * *

ROYAL DOULTON lawnmower. With certificate of provenance and sidecar. £1. WHOft 679.

OVALTEENIES rubberized undersheet for all-night malt drink binges. Plus "I'm an Ovalbedwetter" tin badge. 13/6. FRA2061

SIGNED P.G. Wodehouse first editions. "A Bumming At Blandings", "Leave It To Pbeaver", "Sieg Heil, Jeeves". All good offers considered. SOCkford 910.

HANG ON. Where's my bloomin' dinner? Oi! Where's my bleedin' wife? £1. FRA3961

GEORGE CROSS medal. Unwanted gift. £1 Whoft 5633

WAR SURPLUS Messerschmitt twin tub - 'Ein Volk, Ein Reich, Zwei Tubs!' Insignia and serial numbers filed off. £1. FRAmley 2820.

GUTLESS MESS of a human being hanging

"BUILD YOUR OWN" Build Your Own Kit Kit. Finished! Now it's your turn. 13/6. FRA7332

* * * * * * * * * *
WINNIPEG
* * * * * * * * * *

PRE-FABRICATED husbands to replace those lost or damaged in the war; assemble in seconds. Help rebuild Britain swiftly and neatly. £1, or luxury models from £1. Poulton Pre-Fabricants, FRAmley 4421.

* * * * * * * * * *
DAEDALUS CAKE
* * * * * * * * * *

GASMASKS with flavoured filters. Raspberry, vanilla, Admiral's Pie. Unwanted gift. 10/6 each. WHO4313.

MING VASE. Also Prince Barin punch bowl and Dr Hans Zarkov lobster scissors. £1 each or £1 the set. FRA8553.

CRIKEY! Is that the time? I really should be going, you dreary fat cretin. FRAmley 7409

* * * * * * * * * *
HULA - HULA !
* * * * * * * * * *

BLIND FAITH. Can you afford not to own it? You know you want it. Buy unseen. £1. WHOft 7555

RATION BOOK BINGO full instructions, pens and set of powdered balls. £1. FRAmley 9011.

LADIES' EVENING GLOVE. Strapless evening gown that makes the wearer look like a big glove. Suit single young woman or broadminded couple. £3. FRAmley 5802.

RABBIT'S FOOT umbrella stand. Hard to get your umbrella into, to be honest, but you might just get lucky. £1. FRAmley 5133.

EDWARDIAN CHILD'S ROCKING bookshelves. Covered in HORS

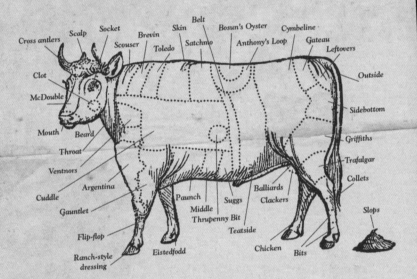

A characteristic Ministry of Meat poster from the late 1940s encouraging the use of Britain's lights and offcut surplus. Though horse and cockthroat had caught on during the war as alternatives to rationed meats, class-conscious Britons were slow to adopt many cheaper cuts, fearful that it might make them look like navvies. Adverts like this were part of a campaign to persuade them otherwards.

Framley World's Fair

In February 1958, the entire West End of Framley town centre was being carefully packed away into storage to make room for an exhibition showing the contribution that Framley had made to world culture.

All that's left of the festival today are memories and a few remaining confused visitors. So let's look back and see what all the fuss must have been about!

Back to our future

It must have been hard to imagine then, looking forward to the future, what we now would be making of the impact that the Framley World's Fair was having at the time.

Although most of the displays concentrated on larger industries such as **fluff milling** and **winkle picking** there was plenty of room for smaller, more localised sectors like mind-blowing, hat-flattening and prostitution.

Next to the main visitors' entrance, a small plot of land was deliberately left undeveloped to show how far construction processes had advanced during the building of the fair. The famous architect, **Sir Edmin Beh**, said of the space - "One can only truly judge one's own progress by comparing it with this tiny square of rubbish."

Functionality was a key selling point for many of the exhibitors. A housing estate was built for the *Framley Roofs and Windows* hall. Utilising exciting new materials such as **chrominium**, **peppersteel** and **Galavantine**, the glass-walled homes were unceremoniously demolished two weeks later to make way for the imposing *Airport Runways of the Future* stand.

The *House of Next Week* exhibit promised visitors a glimpse forty years into the future. Here a Chris Evans sends an electronic letter from his 6-valve television organiser.

A ticket and guidebook from the fair by Framley-ba designer Ibrahim Bethsheveth (both actual size)

Walking along Constitution Walk, visitors the fair would have been confronted with th spectacular *Eyeball of Progress*.

This spherical structure, constructed special for the event, had a long walkway leadin members of the public inside.

A spiral staircase would guide them to the to where a hole with a concave lens wa intended to give an unrivalled view of Framle and environs.

Unfortunately, the eyeball was built starin straight at the sun, rendering most visito blind.

A Tall Order!

The most expensive and striking feature of the fair was the 300 ft high, 10 ft wide 'Tower of Our Tomorrows'.

Originally designed as a freestanding modernist sculpture to complement the 'Bowl of Britishness' - the huge hall that was to house the main exhibits - spiralling costs incurred during construction of the Tower caused the building of the Bowl to be abandoned.

Angry exhibitors, in fear of having to set up their stands in open air or the river Fram, unanimously decided to populate the Tower.

By using the narrow engineering ladders inside the delicate structure for support and allocating six rungs per stand, the 50 tradesmen turned the inside of the Tower into a makeshift miniature exhibition area.

On the opening day, the Tower was so popular with the public that a special airlift service had to be employed to ferry excited people from the top of the structure back down to the beginning of the queue.

The spectacular entrance complex of Framly World's Fair caught in the mid-afternoon on the opening day of the festival.

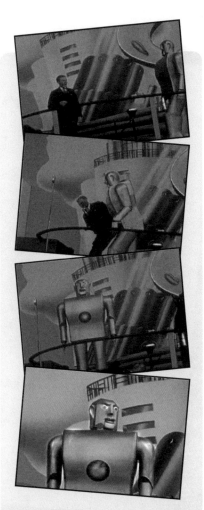

One of the highlights of the exhibition for many was the appearance of **Randy the Robot** at the GEV installation.

The world's first fully automated household dancing robot, Randy was a prototype built by Sockford's Generally Electric Valve company to demonstrate modern micro-engineering techniques.

After being introduced to a packed auditorium by his creator, **Anthony Fonz**, he proceeded to **waltz** across the podium and, to the audience's shock, rectally assault his master.

The metal giant then spoke at some length about job satisfaction and **tap dancing** before bidding the audience farewell and **dismantling** himself.

1956

Time for that
LEMINGTON
feeling!

ONLY *LEMINGTON* REMOVES ALL HAIR

When it's time for that feeling, nothing else will do. Because that feeling is the feeling of confidence you get from a top-of-the-range family shaver. Every mother knows that, if you want to win the germ-war, hygiene demands that your children be clean, full of bacon and bald, bald, bald! More people rely on LEMINGTON than anyone else to keep their children safe. Can you afford not to?

And just look at the gay new things we've done to our shavers! Snap-off clipping trays, faster-than-ever Polar-Tex blades, and FOUR - yes, FOUR! - new stubble-burner settings will keep your kids snooker-ball fresh from the minute they wake up to the moment you put them down. So, remember, when you visit your Electricisatist, ask for LEMINGTON!

Lemington IS PART OF THE GEV GROUP

For the housewife of the 1950s, it wasn't enoug keep her home running smoothly, it had to run cleanly too. New domestic hygiene products flooded the market - cuff bleaches, cistern spr radio fountains - each one promising to kill m germs and remove more filth, often with the stinging new antiseptic power of sage and or

And hygiene didn't just come in a bottle. The relentless march of technology meant that n household cleaning appliances were appear every day. Amongst the most successful wa the Lemington range of family shavers, cas in on the fear of Communist Hair Insects, a produced by the never-sleeping engineers the GEV Company in Sockford.

Though teachers complained that classroc discipline was suffering now that they cou no longer distinguish one hairless, red-fac child from another, the popularity of the Leminton lasted well into the next decade when the arrival of the head-shaking, hai loving Beatle Four made the "egg look" a fashion no-no for the younger generatior

1959

As we approach the 21st Century, it's sad to think that our children of the next millennium may never see a milkman. The decline in the popularity of doorstep delivery has been put down to many factors - increased ramp access to supermarkets; sunspots; rocketing milkman-related murder statistics - but whatever the reason, it's unlikely that our grandchildren will ever see a jaunty poster like this one plastered to the side of a passing post office.

Are you a
silver, yellow
or brown top?

...for full-fat, half-fat
and brown top milk,
just ask your milkman

SUMMER IS HERE...!

... and rationing is over! So why not splash out on the zesty new flavours and keen new household products on offer at **WANDO STORES!**

TRIMMEX GRASS CLIPPINGS

"They're as green as the peas on my plate...!" You loved Trimmex all through the war and beyond as a ration-friendly alternative to vegetables.

So don't forget that great Trimmex taste of natural, garden-fresh grass clippings... Especially now that the man-sized flavour of Trimmex is available at a thrifty new reduced-to-clear price!

2/-
8lb bag

VITA-BOWL OWL PELLETS

1/6
a box

We know you've been waiting for it! You know you've been waiting for it! And it's here! The end of BIRD RATIONING means your favourite Owl Pellets are back on the breakfast menu, with all the regurgitated country goodness Dad loves, all the real brown colour for Mum, and for little Bobby and Janet, the big mousy taste they adore. Contains half your recommended daily allowance of vitamins and fur.

PRINKLE'S "WEEKENDER" TOOTHPASTE

The jet-age formula behind Prinkle's WEEKENDER toothpaste means "Good-By" to pesky bathroom routine! A single brushing with the recommended quantity of Weekender toothpaste lasts 2 whole days (or 6 days in France).

5d
1loz tube
(2 servings)

**JUST IMPORTED...!
EXOTIC FRUITS**

ask
for prices

Bananas ... Colonoscopy Fruit ...
Cariboo ... Golden Difficults ...
Blenheim Perries ... Glenades ...
Diamonds ... Crabflowers ...
Parumpapums ... Grapeapples ...
Catalan Glassberries ...
Red Stripes ... Committee Plums ...
The Lord's Biscuit ... Boules ...
Manor Emerald Spires

LION'S RAY-N-YUMS*

Mmmm! They're tangy! The colourful, hearty food-shaped bites* that keep kids warm and free from germs. NEW!

*contain by-products

8d
a box

Get the big bargains at **WANDO**

1955

1956

THE CODGE TARGETEER

Classifertisements

PEACHES N' PLUMS

FIVE-PIECE VARIETY PACK of cereal. One junior-sized box each of Uf-Os, Jet Flakes, Bikini Atoll Pops, Closet Puffs and Kellogg's Atomicles. 3/-. FRAmley 1167

HAVE YOU NOW or ever been a member of the communist party? Pub Quiz. American Embassy, every Friday. Big career-destroying prizes! Call Joe on FRA8431

TURN YOUR war memoirs into crisps! Good per-word rates. Little Blue Battlefield Anecdote Bags for no extra cost. Call FRAmley 6344 for details.

PROPSHAFT, engine cowling, aileron and wheels from single-seater aircraft. Loft clearance. Also Amelia Earhart. Offers. WHOft 6888

TELEVISION ARIEL. Also gramophone prospero and shortwave caliban. 2 guineas the lot. FRA7110

WILDLIFE BOOK. "The Colourful World Of Penguins". Enormously disappointing. 4/6. SOCkford 588.

STICK of Stanley Matthews Blackpool Rock. Causes excessive dribbling and my teeth have been capped over 100 times. 1/-. FRAmley 7009

ACTION STATIONS

BLONDE bombshells. Army surplus. Assorted ordnance dressed crudely in yellow wigs. Strangely alluring yet incredibly dangerous. Call Col. Colin Callard at RAF Harmonium (xt 2508) btwn 6 and 8am. Details on application.

RUBBLE without a cause. I've just smashed up my fireplace for no real reason. £1. FRA0664

WURLITZER DUKEBOX. Ideal for coffee shops. Delivers all John Wayne's classic lines at the push of a button, and dispenses milk from a horse-shaped siphon. £8. WHOft 763.

LATEST SCORES, news headlines and Suez updates delivered hourly to your hall telephone! Newest ringtones and logos. FRAmley 8633

CUSHION'S Imperial Lather Toilet Soap. Ideal for the sort of people who wash their hands in the toilet. Box of 40. £2. FRAmley 6311

DUNLOP "Wet Weather" vulcanised rubber raindrops. Pack of seven. 18/-. SOCkford 6417

PAIR OF haute couture Givenchy gumboots, as worn by Audrey Hepburn in Prestatyn Holiday. £1 5/6. MOLford 4599.

BED-SITTING room to rent £10 per calendar month. Also toilet-garage and bath-garden. Will not split. FRA1673

VARIETY RICHARD

CONFIDENTIAL information for single people leading to happiness - romance - maybe even death. Write today! Emberly Whunt, Ph.D. Director Personal Services

HALF a hundredweight of Coalex Smokeless Flameless Heatless Coal. Useless bag of black lumps. Doesn't even taste very nice. £offers. FRA6310

"COOL IT, DADDIO!" paternal refrigerator. Keeps Pops on ice whatever the weather! £5. FRAmley 7100

KITCHEN BENDY

PAIR OF absurdly high-waisted trousers with wing collar and epaulettes. Offers. FRAmley 6898

BEATNIK traps. 10/6 ea. Twelve bags of freeform poetry bait. 4/-. MOL9077

STRING of Capstan medium strength Navy Cut sausages. Filterless. "You're Never Alone With A Sausage". 1/6. FRA8663

WHAM BAM-BAMS

COMRADE Stalin's Little Red Book. The Tale of Jeremy Fisher. It's his favourite. 8½d. FRAframley 4555

DELIGHTFUL framed photographs of your children. Framley Zoo, June '55. Blackpool Pleasure Beach, September '57. Paddling pool in your back garden, August '51. Offers. FRA9848

THE SECRET of Successful After Dinner Speaking. 1000s of sure-fire jokes. All hilarious, all in Portugese. "Had them rolling in the aisles" - Lisbon Advertiser. "If I had been Portugese then I'm sure that the evening would have been a great deal more enjoyable" - British Poultry Breeders' Gazette. Call Speechmakers di Porto on WHOft 451.

HOME-MADE chutneys & preserves. Sock jam, shirt pickle, duffelcoat conserve and shoe marmalade. Witness! For now I am wiser. And nude. Prices on application. Dennis. FRAmley 5051

PARPTICUS THE LEOPARD

TWO TICKETS for maiden flight of the "Spirit of St Bernard", experimental subsonic airliner. "An inaudible journey of discovery" - Practical Mechanics Magazine. Offers please to Delores or Branston on FRAmley 3998

COFFEE TABLE, kidney-shaped. Heart-shaped box with restricted left ventricle. Appendix-shaped desk requiring urgent removal before it bursts. £8 the lot. Tel: FRAmley 7339

"MATHS Made Simple" book. 2+6. 2+5. All these and dozens more. £1. FRAmley 9401.

MINI-MITTENS safe cracking gloves. Make your hands as small as keys. Open all doors, safes and bubblegum machines. Great for sexy stuff. 3/- a pair. FRA4019

CHILDREN'S HARDBACK treasury including The Wind-up Willows, Chitty Chitty Kissy Kissy Bond Bond Bang Bang and Charlie & The Chocolate Charlie. Only read four times. 10/6 the lot. FRA7411

BROWNIE UNIFORM, pristine, accessories - hair lice, parachute and spit roast. Also Brownie with 26 badges sewn onto face. Very collectable. Offers. FRA8191

SEWING MACHINE, SINGER, Maria Callas style, once performed Tosca at Covent Garden, some damage from final parapet fall. Offers. FRA6063

THE AMBRIDGE PLAYBARN including screaming Grace Archer costume, inflatable stampeding animals and one book of matches. £2. FRAmley 9599.

GHOSTIES

INDOOR FAIRGROUND. All the miniature fun of the miniature fair in miniature form. Tabletop rollercoaster, Waltzer in your lap, pin three darts in the goldfish and win a dead goldfish. 3 Guineas. WRIpple 725.

AIR VENTS. Massive hit at the Edinburgh Festival. Imagine Marilyn Monroe in the Seven Year Itch wearing a kilt with her meat and two veg out for everyone to see. Now you want one! Call for details. SOCkford 336.

DISPOSABLE CANOE. Use once, then throw away. Used once, hence bargain. 11/3. Framley 5419.

VERY SMALL oval record collection. Rare and unpopular. £10. FRAmley 934.

CAN YOU TELL THE TIME? I can't tell the time! Why can you tell the time? You say half past six! I say flowerpot Keith! Now who's missed this bus? Me. Sockford 688, after 5pm.

BE YOUR OWN BOSS! In just 5 weeks we will teach you how to do a perfect impersonation of your current employer. Box 6541 Whoft.

JAPANESE FIGHTING MICE rare

unusual pets. £

DETECTIVE surpise you never again!

LEV

LIVING MIN as large of because of but as long

ROACH KI bomber. One or your money FRA9445

AROMATIC BEL as far as you can then tighten for because you can! three delightful FRA2433

16MM CAMERA 12mm bottle! I sounds crazy next week tu treatment. WHOf

BINGO MELV

HYPNOTISM for men a You will write to us for Box 7655 Framley.

AMAZING new electric Roto-Motorotome Motorotono-Onomo-Mon Otometer. Startling res for spinning action. Ca out why it rotates? WH

MAKE Money by for notes! As easy as 1 million, 3 million. Our reveals how. FRA6577

PIECES OF EIGHT, sli cutlas cutlets. me FRAmley8755

AUTOMATIC washin Knows exactly when clean your families cl due to being far too c often. Being washed as entirely unpleasant. W

MUSCLES

PREVENT thieves from wallet by disguising it a one pound note. Now y look just like cash! Un unbelievable. WHOft

ODOUR remov by number like t

NEW FOR 195

Techno-Sockford

Framley's beating business heart lies firmly in the heart of Sockford, for it is here that Professor Ernest Skid-Balloon and a shadowy collective of local celebrities established the **Generally Electric Valve Co.**

Responsible for less than or equal to 100% of the world's finest technological advances, GEV were at the forefront of Clement Atlee's valiant, election-losing attempt to replace the entire population of Britain with robots.

Thrusting manfully onwards into the Swinging Fifties and several consequent oscillating decades, GEV's many thumbs in the equivalent number of tasty Business Interest Pies were overseen by Skid-Balloon himself.

The company once belonged to the FTSE (bless you) 100 but on the retirement of Sir Ernest in 1993, a rash investment from the new MD *(see left)* led to huge financial losses and massive redundancies.

In the Science wing you can take a look at some of the GEV innovations that led to a House of Commons enquiry in 1978 if you'd like.

Kalashniasparov

The **Kalashniasparov** was developed in the 1960s to protect Britain from the imminent threat of yet another **chess** Grandmaster emerging from the former (then current) Soviet Union.

Britain hadn't seen a proper chess champion since Fred Perry won at Wimbledon in 1936 and much national pride was resting on the success of the invention.

Using artificial artificial intelligence a **computer** was built that could lose at chess and tie its own **shoelaces** at the same time. With both these functions successfully simulated (thanks to a revolutionary 10% / 90% processing power split in favour of the **shoelaces**), scientists predicted that human British chess players would soon be a thing of the past.

The project was sadly abandoned when the designer of the comptraption, **Jazztim Flunch**, was found hanged in the machine's coils. Flunch had been on the verge of *castling* when the machine took fatal exception and strangled its creator *en passant*.

Though the experiment was classified as a noble **failure**, the research did not go to waste, for without this groundbreaking machine, we would never have had the home Cluedo robot or the digital bow tie.

These three cheeky little **valves** were the first ever made by the Generally Electric Valve Company, in 1941, and were originally used for picking bits of bacon out of Sir Ernest Skid-Balloon's teeth with the pins.

Traffic cones were breeding so prolifically in the 1950s that GEV were tasked with creating a sonic device to render cones impotent. The cone population soon decreased although road accidents soared.

In 1964, a fully-automated **picture of Dorian Gray** was constructed by GEV in conjunction with physicist Arthur Bostrom. Dorian remained the same age until 1978, when the machine got so old that its cogs snapped.

In 1960, the company won the government contract to perform the controlled nuclear explosion that led to the successful formation of the **Orkney Islands**. The area was officially opened by **Oor Wullie** in 1962.

The Fluff Exchange

Framley Fluff Exchange, on the corner of Military Pickle Avenue and Denegate, became to be known as the very centre of what became to be known as **Swinging Framley** in the 1960s. Opened in 1951, as a jazz venue and newsagents, the Fluff Exchange hosted legendary concerts right through the rock and roll boom until it was closed in 1977 because punk had no tunes and you couldn't hear the words. It is now chiefly used as a hole in the ground.

The distinctive
of the Framley
Exchange fell
the sea in 1984
accident with
precedent in
landlocked to

10   ST EVOT'S FLUGEL March 13 1964   ★★★T

BIG NIGHT FOR BEAT

THE TURBOJETS Drummer M. Guitar, leader of the Whoff group, with guitarists C. Drums, B. Trumpets, S. Flutes and singer Michael Notsinging.

STARS OF TOMORROW BEAT EACH OTHER OFF AT FRAMLEY FLUFF EXCHANGE

By RONALD FREFF

IT'S A BIG NIGHT for big beat on Wednesday, as young contenders for the tip top of the top ten do battle at the Fluff Exchange.

Local beat kings from all over the world are all set to deliver a beat-crazy night of beat with the accent on beat.

The contest, sponsored by Babbin's, makers of the fashionable Hit Parader Fishcakes, will include performances by The Turbojets and Rod Lollipop and The Ice Creams.

CRIBBINS

As well as a £1,000 prize, the winning beat combo will get the once in a beat-time opportunity to be the backing band for the recording of Bernard Cribbins' new number-one hit, *On Me Foot*. The session will take place at the studios of top disc-spinners EMI in Penny Lane, where the Beatles are currently recording their new album of George Harrison dropping dice into a glass.

Runners-up all get roof racks for their fathers' cars. The panel the groups have to impress includes Archbishop Makarios, Quintin Hogg, and teen-beat sensation Twiglet.

So what's the time … ? It looks like beat o'clock to me!

FEELING OFF-COLOUR?

Maybe you're not getting enough RED and YELLOW.

Red can be obtained from bacon and paint, yellow from sunshine and bee. Or why not

ROD LOLLIPOP & THE ICE-CREAMS

Many of the groups who passed through the doors of the Fluff Excha went on to fame and fortune or disappeared without tra

...laybill from the 1965s, during the ...ey days of the Exchange features ...enty of familiar names. And even ... years later, all the big faces were ...euing up to appear on the venue's famous revolting stage...

...1976, weathering a slump in their ...pularity, and hoping to net a record ...deal, sixties hitmakers The Beatles ...performed bottom of the bill at the ...Fluff Exchange, underneath up-and-coming pub rock combo Bob Likely ...and The Shovels. Only three people ...ned up, and Paul McCartney was hit, ...peatedly, by a girl's shoe. Five years ...later, John Lennon was shot dead by ...the Dakota Building a sad end to the ...prious career of one of rock and roll's greatest venues.

Radio days!

...he world of radio was shaken to ...s very foundations by the ...nvention, in 1967, of the ...ntrudiode Short Wave ...ienerator, a transmitter that ...roadcast on the resonant ...equency of the human eardrum, ...nabling it to be heard everywhere, ...y everybody, all the time.

...riginally intended as a means of ...nnoying the scientists in the ...uilding opposite GEV's R&D ...epartment, the device, which ...etailed for a very reasonable ...4-3-6 (or £5 in paisley), was ...stantly popular with the cheeky ...ew wave of Burglar Radio DJs.

...hese anarchic characters would ...reak into private homes while ...he owners were out and transmit ...heir wacky shows on the ...ntrudiode without fear of ...ensorship, interference or low ...udience figures, then melt away ...nto the night.

...Vhen the homeowners returned, ...he only evidence that these ...roadcasting buccaneers had ...een in their lounge would be the ...iveaway piles of mugs, pens, ...carves and promotional gonks, ...vhich could often take days to ...lear away.

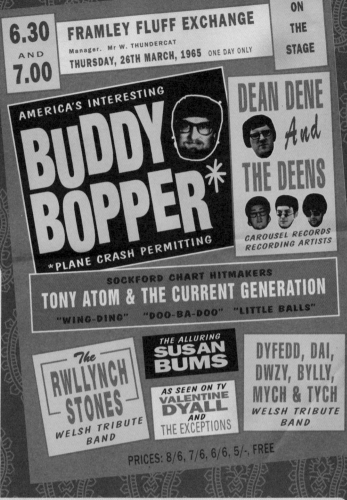

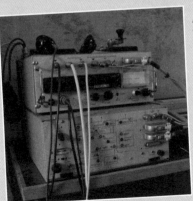

An excellently maintained example of the prototype GEV480 Intrudiode Shortwave Transmitter on display in the Museum's *Swinging Framley* exhibit.

The unit was donated by Mr Alan Clever of the Durbiton Amateur Radio Club and is in full working order, still able to transmit its default high-pitched 11KHz test signal over a 500 yard radius.

If any reader knows of the whereabouts of Mr Clever, we are eager to contact him and find out how to turn his machine off.

1968 the St Eyots Flugel **Classified Adver**

Dutch Cinema

5-BOX VARIETY PACK of contemporary cereals. One portion each of Mindflakes, Mandy Rice Krispies, Beatabix, Satiricles. 1/-. WHOff 743.

ALL MY earthly possessions. Seller emigrating to entirely new headspace. Call Feather on WRipple 621.

SEND ME £20 and I will name a cloud after you or a loved one. Certificate of authenticity and labelled cotton wool picture of your cloud. The perfect gift. FRAmley 0989.

NASTY ROUND of drinks. I thought I wanted them but now I've realised I don't. You know how it is. Birdlime and Soda. Gingham Tonic. Sweat Sherry. Bloody Malcolm. Port Sausage. Lager Bottom. Any takers? Alf on Framley 988.

TURN SIR STAFFORD CRIPPS into a memory. Vote Conservative.

DINKY TOYS Donald Campbell bathtop racetrack. Amazing aerial stunts. Ten spare boats and fishing net. 8/-. FRAmley 8461

CALYPSO HELMET Worn once. No longer either topical or tropical hence 2/6. Contact Lance on FRAmley 4547.

TURN ON. Tune in. Drop scones. The Head Bakery, Whoff. WHO851

Humpty Magnet

HIGH FASHION skis. Unwieldy, uncomfortable, unbelievable. Strapless, peeptoe with stylish rollneck. 13/6. MOL905.

DOVER-TO-CALAIS in 25 minutes, one way. Hovershoes (no other destinations available). Call Christopher on CALais 645.

THERE'S SOMETHING in my eye. Oh yes, I'm sure there's something in your eye too but it's nowhere near as big as what's in my eye. Offers. SOCKford 461.

HABITAT "Prisoner"-style chair. I am not free, I am £6. Also new number 2, will not be flushed. FRA7440

PAIR OF AVANT GARDE trousers. Quite remarkable. Challenging to put on. Thought-provoking to wear.

READER'S DIGEST Book Of The Dead. Includes popular regular features: *It Pays To Increase Your Karmic Balance, Your Inner Child Says The Funniest Things* etc. 13/6. FRAmley 0881

DOG KENNEL, Medium. Some bite marks on interior surfaces, otherwise excellent condition throughout. £3. Would suit child aged 0-5, call Mr Hollyhock on FRAmley 8787.

BABY BIG TEARS. Comes with onion-scented security blanket. 4/-. FRAmley 5570

Bonnets

TRIPLE ALBUM box set. "Boogie Woogie Zurich". The Very Best and All The Rest of Swiss Good Time Rock n Roll. Unwanted gift. 11/-. FRA6704.

VICTORIAN effect celery grinders. Pair of three. 9/6. FRA6851

 Missed a bargain in last week's ST EYOTS FLUGEL Classifieds Section?

Not to worry. The *St Eyots Flugel* duplicates all **For Sale** items so your bargain may still be in stock at our warehouse.

Call FRAmley 7676

HALLOWE'EN costume. Looks exactly like Liza Minnelli will look in 35 years' time. Chills the blood. £1 11/6. FRA8404.

PARALYMPIC-STANDARD pole-vault pole. Will support the weight of most wheelchairs. £2. MOLford 490

CELEBRITY dental work. Teeth removed. Wisdom a speciality. It hurt and he deserved it. He was hopeless in *The Early Bird*. FRAmley 3018

CAN YOU tell the difference between Stork SB and Pepsi Cola? Then come round and make my tea, my wife's rubbish. WHOff 206.

TRANSCENDENTAL MEDITATION for really stubborn, pig-ignorant and stupid people. Feel the healing power of ommmm

doors which appear to be sealed by some sort of Egyptian curse. Contents unknown. Offers to Miriam on FRAmley 643.

Sinatra Oil

EXPERIMENTAL DRUG. Most users experience brief euphoria followed by sensation of being married to Leonard Bernstein. US Army surplus (Operation Rolling Thunder, N. Vietnam). £3 a barrel. FRAmley 2887.

PACKS OF Smiths' Plasters. Salt 'n' Vinegar flavoured. "Don't rub salt in the wound... Rub Salt 'n' Vinegar in!" Really hurt. 1s. FRA7200

SENATOR PAUL MCCARTNEY'S "Witchhunt" game. Can you be first to burn Yoko Ono at the stake? 11/6. MOLford 501.

ALL THE bits from inside a lady. Kept refrigerated in airtight Tupperware containers (not included). Misunderstanding on first date. 3 guineas the lot. Chutney 568.

THE ROYAL FRAMLEY OBSERVATORY. Set of 6 images from our new radio telescope :- ceiling / lens cap / coffee swirling in a cup / swan passing / Orion Nebula obscured by trainee astronomer's eye / woman across street trapped in a bra. Good prices. Call Dr Borglesham at the RFO on FRA 6419

VACUUM CLEANER, Hoover. Full of chicken grease, feathers and me, otherwise as new. £2. FRAmley 8304

SPIKE MILLIGAN hiding in the boot of a Rolls Royce. Peter Sellers to collect. £1. FRA9651

I'm coming

PEACE BEADS, 8d per million, Dave Hip, tel Whoff 68834

SIGNED WORLD CUP 1966 leather football. Genuine. Geoff Hurst, Gordon Banks and Patsy Rowlands hence £1. FRA3505.

HOPELESS AT MAKING SEX? Let us help you. Relaxing and mind-broadening treatments available, with some rimming and fisting. Call the Rodox Cent... Framley...

LAWN MOWER, Suffolk Punch, £7. Also Glasgow Kiss, £5, may require some stitches. Call Framley 3336.

RAILWAY RELICS wanted by collector. Station signs, clocks, lamps, smoke, Edwardian passengers, Dr Beeching's balls in an eggcup would be great. Good prices paid. Call Michael on WHOff 902

YOU'RE PRETTY but you're not that pretty, you're funny but you're not that funny, you're clever but you're not that clever and you're thin but you're not that thin. 1001 Classic "You're Dumped" One Liners. Call Lynne on CODge 640.

DOES YOUR SON suffer from wet dreams? Send us a photograph of either parent and we will provide you with a permanently "on-the-soft" That's Better™ pillow. Affordable and effective. Sandpit & Sons Ltd. FRAmley 981.

DO YOU WANT a cup of tea? One sugar? Sorry. This one's got two in it. Offers? MOLford 6106

Crows and gulls

DOG MOUSTACHES. Mouse beards. Cow eyebrows. Latest styles and old favourites, all genuine pet hair. Make your cat look like Boss Cat, but in disguise. Pricelist on request. FRA5117

WALLPAPER with "Hidden Faces" design. Great for nervous kids. 3/6 a roll. Wripple 409.

ASSORTED confectionery. Pack of Bassett's Dolly Birds, Limited edition Jimi Hendrix Star Spangled Spangles (covered in burning petrol), Carnaby Bars. Call the 1910 Fruitgum Co. on Fram 879.

JOB LOT of bottles of 3-in-1 "Head & Elbows" Shampoo, conditioner and mayonnaise. Cleans greasy hair, making it soft and manageable, then makes it greasy again. A shilling a bottle. FRAmley 308.

HELP! I need money to fund my shit play! Would you like to help support my pointless self-delusion? Then send money to help me stage my shit play! Box FE6455.

LITTLE ONES? Yes! The...

* MR. HITCHCOCK WISHES TO KINDLY REMIND HIS AUDIENCE THAT NO ONE... BUT NO ONE...WILL BE ALLOWED INTO THE AUDITORIUM TO SEE HIS NEW FILM

ALFRED HITCHCOCK'S

SAUSAGES

CERT X

STARRING

CELEBRITY	AVIARY	SPIRAL
BUTTER	**QUILLS**	**HEIDI**

Alfred Hitchc..?

and ALFRED **HITCHCOCK** as MR. GUFFS

1960 Cinema underwent another boom period in the swinging decade. This poster for the summer of 60's smash-hit suspense thriller shows how adept directors had become at teasing and delighting their audiences. Other tricks to make the cinemagoer sit up and take notice included electric shocks wired through their ice cream, real murders in the auditorium synchronised to the murders on screen, and making the films really good.

When Psychedelia hit Framley in 1967's glorious summer of love, it was the older residents who dug the new groove first. While youngsters were still feeling the vibe of milk-house culture, Norman Wisdom chic and trad barbershop on vintage wax, the pensioners found themselves a whole new scene that was beamed direct to the third eye from somewhere totally other.

1968

The enthusiastic uptake of freak culture by Framley's senior citizens was blamed on many factors, but perhaps most significant was the presence in town of the Framley Twilight Home for Retired Gentlefolk, an institution which, according to the real together heads, had access to the best supply of recreational sedatives in Western Europe.

The graphic design of this poster reflects the concerns of those thrilling days when anything seemed possible if you were old.

Here Comes the Railways!

Before there were trains, there were no trains. By **1800**, smoggy Framley was awash with horses and cartses and expertses predicted that within ten years, horses in the town's streets would be up to their eyebrows in drivers' dung. (Due to an obscure bye-law)

The beginning

In 1810 the perpetually sitting mayor, **Obfusciah Aintree**, commissioned a study which concluded that the high level of traffic in the area was probably caused by the absence of roads into or out of the town. With no way of leaving Framley and growing housing problems he proposed two options

i) the building of a rail link to "somewhere beyond"

or

ii) the erection of another layer of town above the present town.

The double-decker town was immediately commissioned, and built within six months. Having divided the residents into "upper" and "lower" classes it was just a short while before complaints were pouring in from the lower orders about the noise of hooves galloping on the new brass roads upstairs.

The Framley riot of 1815 is fondly remembered by those who died.

By 1815 tinnitus had become an endemic problem and, after a shire horse fell through some temporary roadworks on the first floor killing several orphans below, riots followed with separatists finally destroying the upper tier in a colourful explosion with the loss of many lives.

Into the future...?

The train never stands still, they say, and a proposed new **rail link** for Framley is set to prove them right, whoever they are.

The space-age rail link will connect the town of Framley directly to the future. New **magnetic engines** that travel faster than the speed of time will allow people to arrive at their destination hundreds of years after they leave Framley Parkway station.

The system's inventor, **Professor Arthur Bostrom** warns that the timetable will be extremely strict, and return journeys to the present will only arrive back at the original departure date if the engines travel *slower* than the speed of time. Trains leaving late from the future will arrive back before they left to get there, except unless (hang on, he explained this to me in the pub with the cruet set and two glasses, but I've forgotten it now)

The railway

After the **failure** of the double-decker town, the call went out for someone who could somehow relieve Framley's traffic problems.

Untangling this knot of transport was an engineering feat that would test the resolve of the greatest minds of the age, and not a job for the faintheaded.

It would take the genius of one man to bring the railway to Framley, and that man was **Dave** (later Sir Dave).

Dave

Within two years, horse-drawn steam engines known colloquially as the **horse and iron horse** trotted around the town under art of the state of the art viaducts that could be elevated to allow top hats to pass underneath. Soon Framley was knee deep in dung once more. This was the dawn of the railway age!

A Look Under The Bonnet of Cars

There's nothing that gets me warm under the collar more than the prospect of being in a red-hot car. And Framley has played its place in that history, thanks to the Sockford Motor Works and their tireless quest for speed or comfort. Due to reasons of space, I'm

...re's how cars have evolved naturally over the last million years, from primitive man with his feet to modern man with his places to go... in a car!

Crack designer

No figure looms larger over Framley's motoring golden age than **Sir Alec Issinoho**, racing driver, boulevardier, and chief stylist for Sockford Motor Works.

As a young man in his 1920s, Sir Alec had experimented with the external combustion engine - the groundbreaking new system in which the combustion of the fuel happens *outside* the engine, in the driver's cupped hands. This led to him losing all his hair at the age of seventeen, and gave him his distinctive lopsided wave.

By the early '30s, he had already designed two popular cars for SMW - the mighty *Velociraptipator D-Class* and the *Garibaldi Tourer* - both sporting his trademark big front wheel and tiny back wheel, a hangover from his tenure as chief stylist at the recently defunct Molford Bicycle Works.

Addicted to speed

Issinoho retired in 1947 and, inspired by Gordon Properly's shattering of the existing **land speed record** (which had stood at 9 since 1911), dedicated his life to beating the quickness barrier. Between 1947 and 1966, Sir Alec built six experimental vehicles, each one with a more massive engine, but always his attempts fell just short of Properly's record.

In 1969, however, he cracked it. By caving into pressure from his support crew and replacing the vast 18-foot front wheel with one the same size as the back wheel, wind tunnel tests seemed to indicate his latest vehicle - *Blue Riband* - would be able to break the record.

On July 11th, Issinoho strode across the test track at the Urling Salt Flats, climbed into the tiny cabin of his bullet-shaped car and gunned the engine. At the drop of the flag, he released the clutch and the vehicle leapt forward.

Unfortunately, the new level-bodied car was now so powerful that it raced off without Sir Alec in it, circumnavigated the globe and smacked him in the back of the head, killing him instantly before his buttocks had even touched the ground.

His posthumous record stands to this day.

Framley in the 1960s: the three-way system

By the 1960s, **Framley**, like most English towns, was becoming choked with traffic. The greatest challenge facing town planners was how to deal with what poet laureate **Sir John Benjamin** called *"the dread motor-car, that burping boxy nincompoop."*

In 1962, an expensive team at Framley Borough Council came up with a revolutionary system to move the 68,000 vehicles a week more efficiently around the town: the three-way system. Trials of the system using miniature traffic proved a great success, and the new three-way system was opened in June 1963 by the leader of the council, **Sir Alphabet Morecambe**.

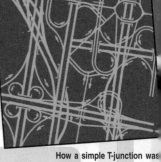

How a simple T-junction was modified to become a modern three-way junction.

(Reprinted by permission Framley Highways Department / Saatchi Collection)

The only car I ever owned, a Morris Traveller. My first widow and I went round Europe in it, getting as far as the ferry before the seats caught fire and it was written off. I still have the wheels in my loft.

The incredibly complicated road layout, however, was beset with difficulties from the start. On the first day, 300 confused vehicles ended up in a giant knot. To this day, eight drivers have never been found.

The rules were complicated, and frequently changed. When the system opened, for example, although the road-user could drive either side of the oncoming traffic, lane-switching was strictly forbidden.

This proved unpopular in the long term, because people who got on the wrong side of the opposing traffic could end up taking diversions of up to 29 miles in order to get to the place 500yds away that they had originally wanted to reach in the first place in the beginning.

In 1971, the system was simplified with the addition of a multi-storey roundabout, but after 15,000 deaths attributed to the scheme, it was all rubbed out and started again by Mayor D'Ainty in 1976. The streets of Framley are now colour-coded depending on where they go and how they get there.

Framley in mid-air

If it's alright with you I'd like to speak a little about the exciting history of air travel within Framley.

So fasten your cigarette and extinguish all of your seatbelts as we take a cursory glance at Sockford Aerodrome!

Not many people are aware that the land beneath **Sockford Aerodrome** was used for flight long before the dawn of the plane age.

The main runway was originally built in 1893 to allow steam trains to build up the speed necessary for jumping the valley of the River Sock, but despite a flurry of interest in the 1920s, aeroplanes never really took off at the site.

In 1942, however, the land was utilised by the **United States Army Air Force** for target practice. After a few weeks' bombardment, the earth was flattened to such an extent that it made an excellent platform for planes to take off from, and so an airport was born.

This picture of Sockford Aerodrome taken in 1971 shows the main control tower, on top of which air traffic controllers would stand and shout directions at incoming planes (this was later replaced by a radio system). A couple of years later an experimental level crossing was suspended 100ft above the terminal to control the flow of air traffic onto the airport's revolutionary single runway, designed at 90º to be Europe's shortest and widest.

Winter of 1953 saw the runway covered in sheet ice. The lack of friction demanded a great deal of skill from the pilots to land. Planes would overshoot their landings in dazzling displays of grace and athleticism that always impressed onlookers.

The site fulfilled a secondary function during wartime; as a repository for the nation's **deaf**. On April 3rd 1943, all the deaf people in Britain were requisitioned at gunpoint and placed for safekeeping in a salt mine beneath Sockford Aerodrome. **Sir Hubert Windpipe**, MP for Framley During The War, explained the situation to me in an interview I once saw.

"The deaf had to be kept safe because they couldn't hear air raid sirens. We had tried visual warnings, such as releasing clouds of colourful balloons, but this just attracted enemy bombers."

"England without the hard-of-hearing would have been unthinkable. We had to preserve the Great British 'Pardon?'"

The scheme was a roaring success, with every deaf person in Britain safely underground by April 5th. Unfortunately, as a prime military target, the aerodrome was bombed two days later killing everyone.

Due to unpopularity, Sockford's arrivals lounge fell into disuse and in 1972 was turned into a **theme pub**, *'The Arrival'* where people could get a stiff drink before flying.

For a while the airport operated a Departures Only policy until they ran out of planes. In the first ten years of operation the aerodrome had only one arrival, who left immediately, after stealing a couple of magazines.

To this day, local residents still use Sockford Aerodrome as their number-one port of call when they want to go away. In fact, it's still flying high today!

In **1976** its familiar yellow doors were painted orange.

SPACE CHUNKS

they're out of your world!

FREE!

Dinosaurs of the Past
collect all three

Ptacptactil, Stegorarasaurus or the Trex
Which one will you get in your dinner?

What better way to wake up in the morning than with a steaming plate of all-new Space Chunks from Milburn's?

With real chunks of meat goodness and our own special coloured sauce, you can guarantee that every spoonful is giving your child what they need to go into orbit.

You can see it's a Millburn's Meal!

Milburn's
SPACE
Chunks
IN SAUCE

1966 Interest in the Space Race meant if you wanted kids to eat something, it had to come from space! Milburn's also made the popular Instant Egg Mustard, which they claimed had been used to fill Sputnik.

To *boldly* *to go: Framley in Space*

 The timeless worlds of space were one of Framley's first final frontiers. In 1952, amateur rocketry enthusiast **Professor Arthur Bostrom** and a team from **Framley Engineering College** launched the town's first manned space mission, to the top of Mount Everest.

The summit of the forbidding Nepalese mountain was chosen as a destination because it was far too far to walk, and on 1th February that year, spacenaut **Uri Nettleton** and sherpa **Toksvig Runway** blasted off in their rocket, the *Saucy Space Nancy*.

Their three-day visit didn't last long however, and on their return it was suggested by the police and others that the whole mission had been faked. Amongst evidence cited in the three-month fraud trial of *Regina v. Bostrom et al* (1955) was footage in which the mountain appeared to flap in the wind and a photograph of the reflection in Nettleton's helmet showing a row of shops and a man in a cardigan getting off a bus.

After four days of deliberation, the jury was unable to reach a verdict, and Bostrom walked free. Nettleton died of a heart attack on the eve of the trial, and Runway ran away, so no-one can really answer the question of whether man really went to Everest in a rocket powered by a sewing-machine motor.

Bostrom has always denied any fraud. At the time, he told the court that he had no respect for the claims of his accusers. "These people aren't scientists. That's what it's like at the top of Everest. The air is so thin that mountains flap in the wind, and the sun reflected in the sky can look like a row of shops and a man in a cardigan getting off a bus."

The rocket, which was rubbish, is now in the children's playground at Framley museum.

ABOVE: The *Saucy Space Nancy* in its final resting place. Please do not play on it, because it still works.

LEFT: Some badge or other.

IN THE CORNER: Even kids got involved with this ludicrous waste of money by bothering their parents for ludicrous wastes of money like these sticks of Space Rock.

News of the 70s!

When a panel of experts was asked in 1978 to name *"The Decade of the Year"*, they all agreed - The 1970s!

And they were right, because as these clippings from the Framley Examiner archives show, the times they were a-ch-ch-ch-changing!

When, in 1977, the Amalgamated Union of Baker's Hat Manufacturers downed tools in dispute over new Common Market hat height guidelines, breadmakers tried their best to struggle on. But within a week, the loose-baker's-hair content of loaves was in excess of Department of Health guidelines and bread manufacture had to be halted outright. In the meantime, as this thin clipping shows, housewives were urged to do their best to improvise.

WHOFT SENTINEL & ADVERTISER   10th of June, 1974

ZEPHYR ON THE AIR!

By NEWSPAPER KIPPS

There's a new radio station in town and that radio station is Zephyr AM and that town is this town, Framley!

Following governmental pressure on local pirate station Radio Deirdre, Postmaster General Edward Ward Edwards has requested that the commercial licenses be granted to enable a new 'Music Service' for the Framley Area. Radio Deirdre, which has been broadcasting illegally from a hot air balloon tethered above Whoft for the last 3 years, has been attracting record listening figures with its groundbreaking mix of popular music and music.

Wacky Zephyr AM star Kenny Plate shows us his crazy side again.

TUNE IN

The new station, Zephyr AM, will be hosted by names familiar to fans of Radio Deirdre. The first few presenters have already been chosen; Adrian Galleon, Kenny Plate, Simon Megadeth, Tenby and The Colonel, and microphone pioneer Ron Bovril. The all-important breakfast show will be helmed by Radio Deluxe's self-styled "mister mornings" Harry Cornflake.

Tenby and The Colonel were blasély optimistic about their move to Zephyr AM, "It's nothing new, dear. We've been knocked around schedules more times than we've been given new shows to present," they shouted to me as I was climbing down Deirdre's rope ladder.

As one of his shoes narrowly missed my head, the Colonel told me he was convinced the twosome have been snapped up because of their enviable demographic: a typical Tenby and The Colonel listener is 70% female, the ideal target audience for the new commercial franchises.

Here's how to assemble your ZEPHYR AM *Schedule Mobile*

You'll never need to miss your favourite shows with our fact-filled ZEPHYR AM SCHEDULE MOBILE!

The gently spinning faces of ZEPHYR AM's star Disc Jockeys make it child's play to plan your radio listening on ZEPHYR 1375 AM!

1974 saw the birth of Framley's longstanding longwave favourite, Zephyr AM. With its line-up of top new presenters stolen from another station, and its lively new approach of *"Hit After Hit After A Word From Our Sponsors"*, Zephyr AM quickly picked up a fanatical following - so fanatical that by 1978 each and every one of its DJs was being stalked by fat, metally unstable women in Zephyr AM sweatshirts. Tenby and The Colonel never married.

ST EYOT'S FLUGEL September 15th, 1977   PAGE

HOW YOU CAN BEAT THE BREAD CRISIS!

by BRITTANY GRANADA

THOUGH THE queues are enough to make anyone give up eating altogether, madam – you can still do something to make life a little better during the current bread shortage.

You could always, of course, cut it out of the family diet completely. Doctors inform me that there would be no harm in doing so in today's over-fed society.

In fact, of course, given the fact that over a third of today's children are clinically obese in fact, you might be doing them a favour in fact.

Bread can always be replaced in the school lunch by other foods – hamburgers, cheeseburgers, butter, suet or animal rennet. Liven up their lunchboxes by using raisins or chocolate buttons to make a happy rabbit's face in a teacup-full of drippping and your children will forget they ever asked for sandwich spread.

And don't forget other alternatives.

Try **Paper Oatcakes** – which you can butter like bread. For four you need:

2lbs of cooked sieved, shredded newspaper; 3oz. porridge oats; 1 tsp proprietary brand salt; little gravy to bind.

METHOD: *Roll the ingredients into a ball and serve on greased coasters.* Or if you're in a hurry,

just cut this recipe out and eat it. Remember to rememberise the recipe before you do so.

For a teatime treat why not serve the family some **Flour-free pancakes**? – and they-make a great breakfast idea too!

8 eggs; 0oz flour; a little salt; tbsp oil; milk.

METHOD: *Break the eggs carefully into a frying pan full of hot oil. Do not add the milk. Add salt to taste. Makes eight delicious, savoury, white and yellow pancakes.*

Serve with sausages, bacon, grilled tomatoes and two fried slices of bread. Delicious!

Bread-free Bread & Butter Pudding

USE the usual recipe, just omitting the bread,

The 1970s were a time to pass the mourning of old traditions, and welcome a new century - the 1980s!

Language dies with last living speaker

Old tongue is finally put out of misery

News EXTRA
Night watch

SPY cameras are to be installed in policemen in Framley as part of an initiative to stop the beat coppers being hijacked and driven away by gangs of youths. The move follows an incident where a burnt out officer in the approach road to the FR404 held up traffic for several days.

By ARCADY BELVEDERE

THE LAST REMAINING living speaker of an ancient local tongue has died, his family announced this week.

Banbury Riggers, who was 108 in February, passed away peacefully in his socks on Wednesday evening, said his daughter Chastise.

Mr Riggers was the only extant speaker of Wrellych, a 900-year-old

Mr Riggers in 1912

dialect once mildly popular in parts of the region. Wrellych has similarities with Moroccan, Middle Estuary and Nonsense.

Speakers of Wrellych numbered less than a boxer's dozen by 1911, according to records in the British Library, and when Mr Rigger's wife Beyoncé died in 1964, he found himself in the Guinness Book of Records as its only speaker worlwide.

Mr Rigger, who was famously interviewed by Roger Stilgoe on Nationwide, was surrounded by his daughter when his soul departed.

His headstone will be embossed with his chosen epitaph . . . *Grog Sollow Fi Burst* (live today, die today, live today, die today, something something tongue armour).

G.35

Local business is open for business

Petrol By Post a "roaring success"

by TAUNTON MISHAP

A "PETROL BY POST" SCHEME set up by two brothers from Wripple has yet again proved itself a roaring success!

For the sixth time this month, Framley sorting office was razed to the ground by fire in the early hours of Tuesday morning. Firemen in crimson appliances found themselves in attendance.

Duty Manager Frank Bleasdale, 47 next July, described how the inferno took hold of the newly-rebuilt office.

"At around 1.30am in the middle of the night," he once upon a timed, "fire broke out in the sorting racks by the ice-cream machine, and quickly took hold of the Victoria Place corner of the building.

"Fortunately, this is now second nature to us, and the entire staff was successfully evacuated." He also added, off the record, that the GPO is seeking a meeting with the management of Petrol By Post to explore the terms of an agreement about not sending explosive fluid in paper envelopes

TAG > clipping caption XXXXXX god knows what julie is going to drag out of that pile of old newspapers but get simon to bung something in here XXXXXXX

The Framley Poster Service

In **1971**, in response to the most dangerous summer since records began, a special department of Framley Council was set up to raise public awareness of safety, community and political issues. Their distinctive posters and advertisements, and later films, set new standards for new standards, and are remembered fondly by anyone who grew up at that time.

Here we present a couple too many of them.

DON'T GO WITH BAD STRANGERS (1978)
Designed by Morton Lams, Framley Poster Service. ▶

Don't go with bad strangers

No-one minds if you go with good strangers, but you could get in all sorts of trouble if you go with bad strangers, such as an ice cream man with a tattoo. If you get home, check with Mum or Dad what sort of stranger you were with.

Issued on behalf of FBC by
the Framley Poster Service

There's a wealth of knowledge at your local.

Drink and Learn at your Local Pub

THERE'S A WEALTH OF KNOWLEDGE AT YOUR LOCAL (1980)
Designed by Zeron Di Pends, Framley Poster Service.

CHUNKY SAYS... (1974)
Designed by Esilabeth McLibrary, Framley Poster Service. ▶

Part of the famous "Chunky" campaign. An horrific series of accidents in late 1973 were blamed on the character when stress of overwork caused the cartoon cat to offer erratic and dangerous advice, voiced by well-loved local radio DJ Kenny Plate.

Chunky says...•

"Ignore my last public information film, I'd had rather a long day."

If you've been tempted to follow Chunky's advice from the public information film which aired on the evening of July 53rd, 1974, please think again. Chunky wishes it to be known that he'd had "rather a long day" and his recommendations reflected this. Pylons are not fun to climb, and can in many cases be dangerous. Don't try flying your kite near them.

WATCH OUT, WATCH OUT THERE'S A LITTER THIEF ABOUT!

WATCH OUT, WATCH OUT... (1975)
...signed by Esilabeth McLibrary, Framley Poster Service.

...other popular poster by Framley graphic designer and inventor of the ...e vault, Esilabeth McLibrary. In order to make children aware of the ...blem of litter theft, the Poster Service chose to use the striking colour ...eme popularised by national hero Kevin Keegan, with his famous red-...d-white striped pyjamas.

Clunk Clique every week

Try to wear your seatbelt at least once a week. Tests prove that wearing a seatbelt can drastically impair your ability to cause accidents.
So, come on! Join the **CLUNK CLIQUE!**

The wearing of seatbelts is not yet compulsory in the UK, but using a restraining belt could save your life in the event of an accident or collision. Remember, it's your face and you've only got one of them, so try and look after it rather than doing your level best to shred it to ribbons as you cannon through the windscreen of your Hillman Avenger. You don't want to look like some kind of hideous meat-faced freak, now, do you?

CLUNK CLIQUE (1977)
Designed by Bunny Spentence, Framley Poster Service.

Fronted by TV star Terry Ordinary, in his role as down-at-heel car-thief-cum-detective Eddie Shoes from the ratings-topping series *"Shoes' Clues"*, this hugely effective safety drive reduced horrific accidents in the town centre by a percent.

...on't walk on the ...racks in the ...avement!

If possible don't walk on the pavement at all. You wouldn't walk on the pavement at home so why do it in the street?

ISSUED BY THE FRAMLEY POSTER SERVICE

DON'T WALK ON THE CRACKS (1976)
Designed by Osmo Welsh, Framley Poster Service.

This short-lived poster was issued in January 1976 on behalf of the Framley Highways Dept to reduce wear and tear on footpaths after their annual repair budget ran out.

POWER THROUGH UNITY (1973)
Designed by Karennah Biske, Framley Poster Service.

The Service's involvement in William D'Ainty's victorious 1973 electoral campaign was well rewarded. Office reallocation in 1974 netted every employee of the agency their own electric coffee sharpener and a full-sized desktop swimming pool.

D'AINTY

POWER THROUGH UNITY

This is the Age of the Syntheziser

Computers aren't just used for tying your shoelaces or eating your eggs, they can also be programmed to make robotic music.

I would think that every record of the last 30 years has got a **synthesiser** on it and each of these instruments was probably based on the technology pioneered by Sockford's **Generally Electric Valve Co** and their **Mr. Peter Moutarde**.

1959

The **Moutarde 1B** was the first instrument able to fully, albeit quietly, reproduce the sound of an entire orchestra.

Inside it were dozens of **tiny instruments** including cellos, timpani and a miniature baby grand piano, all led by a footswitch-controlled clockwork conductor.

The project was soon scrapped after a work associate of Moutarde went mad whilst attempting to construct an oboe the size of a cigarette.

Popular 1970s duo *Texture* released a hit album of classical compositions played entirely on the Moutarde 2X

In 1966 the **Moutarde 2X "Cordless"** electric syntheziser was released. A series of complaints led to its hasty withdrawal and replacement with the **Moutarde 2X "Corded"** which, unlike its predecessor, could be plugged in to a wall socket and switched on.

The most important discovery of Moutarde's career came in 1973 when he discovered that he could trigger prerecorded sounds from a synthesiser keyboard. He explained his technique thus;

"In the same way that one might catch a fart in a jar to enjoy later, we can capture any sound from one moment, and replay it at another moment of our choice."

197X

Excited by the possibilities of the new technique, Moutarde quickly constructed a prototype, the **Moutarde 3X SoundFellow**.

On completion, the synthesiser had the engineers spellbound. The sounds eminating from it were described as ranging from *"crisp bassoons"* to *"percussive horns"*, as well as one unspecified setting known merely as *"the noise"*, which was scientifically measured as the most beautiful thing that had ever happened in the history of the earth.

At a press conference held a month later to launch the instrument journalists were less complimentary about the 3X's tonal capabilities, likening the sound to *"a load of old bees"* .

MUSIC MACHINE STILL SOUNDS LIKE BEES

by our reporters U. Cloybeam with P. Clutchstraw

BUZZ! BUZZ! BUZZ! BUZZ! BUZZ! BUZZBUZZ! TURN IT OFF!!

At a presconference today at Moutarde Technologies, their flagship new synthesising piano was unveiled to a chorus of journalistic disapproval.

Although we were promised a full orchestral display, what we got was, quite frankly, a bloody disgrace.

Though my scientific companion seemed fascinated by the mechanism, I couldn't hear a

Reporters of the time were unimpressed by the Moutarde 3X's revolutionary new sound.

Further investigation by Moutarde into the problem revealed the problem - a nest of bees had made their way through the speaker grille at the front and made their home between the fan and water pump.

"The bees", Moutard explained at the time, *"were attracted by the special lubricant that we use in the Moutarde 3X."*

Sure enough, the bees seemed to have taken a liking to the **sixty eight gallons of honey** that the machine required to keep a steady Middle C.

The 8-day Week

In February 1973, with the national economy spiralling towards meltdown and people's lights going on and off all the time, Framley had problems of its own. The town's overgrown population was working too hard, there were too many jobs being done too well, and the local economy was in danger of overheating or boiling up. Binmen had started to pile up in the streets, and the situation was nearing criticality.

The Town Hall's solution was to introduce the 8-day week. The eighth day, **Odinday** (like the other days of the week, named after a Norse dog) came between Thursday and Friday, so as not to spoil the weekend.

1973	EASTER				1973	
			Friday	Saturday	It's Sunday	Monday
Tuesday	Wednesday	Thursday	Odinday	**4**	**5**	**6**	**7**
1	**2**	**3**	**3**				
Tuesday	Wednesday	Thursday	Odinday	Friday	Saturday	It's Sunday	Monday
8	**9**	**10**	**10**	**11**	**12**	**13**	**14**
Tuesday	Wednesday	Thursday	Odinday	Friday	Saturday	It's Sunday	Monday
15	**16**	**17**	**17**	**18**	**19**	**20**	**21**
Tuesday	Wednesday	Thursday	Odinday	Friday	Saturday	It's Sunday	Monday
22	**23**	**24**	**24**	**25**	**26**	**27**	**28**
Tuesday	Wednesday	Thursday	Odinday	Friday			
29	**30**	**31**	**31**	**?**			

...es of Molford

At great expense to ratepayers, the BBC was hired to make-up and broadcast an extra day's **television news** to the area once every eight days (or once every week on an 8-day calendar). The fictional news slot, *"New News"*, lasted just 15 weeks (or 13 weeks and a day on an 8-day calendar) and was largely judged a success, although *The Daily Telegraph* criticised one broadcast which suggested that Harold Wilson had eaten Tom and Jerry on a plate.

Framley police's successful "1970s Badge Amnesty" emptied ...dreds of clay pots on sideboards and cleared the back parts of ...usands of drawers in the Framley area. The haul was donated ...e museum in 1988 and is now housed in an enormous clay pot ...e South corridor, together with Britain's largest collection of ...ign coins with holes in them.

Cartoonists of the day, such as Plum from the St Eyot's Flugel, poked genital fun at the crisis.

"Mary! There's a small boy in my pipe who wants to know why he's got to go to school 6 days a week!"

Do you remember?

Trainers that looked like plimsolls
Pink school caviar
Smoking cigarettes behind a policeman
Leo Sayer landing on the moon
Everything being cheaper than it is now
Remembering the 1950s
Horses boycotting the Grand National
The Internet in newspaper form
School fieldtrips to your back garden
Finding a 'Golden Tiger' in your cereal
Paul Newman in that cowboy film
Crying yourself to sleep
Printing your own money
Scientists losing the cure for baldness
Meat Monitors
Instant Ice Granules
National Mahogany Awareness Month
The first mobile phone (with 8 mile cord)
Pirates sabotaging the University Boat Race
Pound Chews

What do you want to be when you grow up?

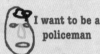 I want to be a policeman

I want to be a lolly

 I want to be an eyebrow

I want to be a robber

I want to be Batman's hair

I want to be a hexagon

 I want to be a milkman and an astronaut

 I want my mum

 I want to be the back half of a cello

I want to be boiling hot

 I want to be the civil service

I want to be CLS Operations Analyst at IBM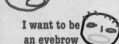

I want to be invisible to radar

I want to be the Prime Minister's wizard

I want to be a woman

I want to be an eyebrow

I want to be the Big Bing Bong on the Bing Bang Bong

I want to go higher on the swings

I want to be an eyebrow

I want to be phenomenal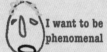

I want to be red in the rainbow

I want to be a Careers Advisor

We can't all be what we want to be, but we can be someone who tells people who can't be what they want to be what they can be.

Ask your Careers Advisor about careers as a Careers Advisor

Give a pinta blooda day

The next time that you have a fatal accident, just remember that it could be *anyone's* blood that the doctor slaps back into your veins.

If you'd rather have an arm full of your own, then giving just *one pint* a day will increase the chances of receiving your own blood back again.

It's your bloody duty

The National Blood Transfusion Service

1975

Ever since its discovery at the turn of the century, blood had remained an uncertain and mysterious science until comprehensive research was undertaken at the Sockford-based MacTavish Institute in the early 1960s. A regional blood bank was quickly established although scandal hit almost immediately when its first bank manager was dismissed for failing to advise loan recipients that their blood could be coagulated if they failed to keep up repayments.

Reserve stocks were at an all-time low when a new campaign was devised in 1975. It is thought that this particular poster may have been inspired by a classic episode of Galton & Simpson's popular television programme *Steptoe & Son*, in which Harold chose to die rather than receive an urgently needed transfusion of his father's blood.

The new pint-a-day personal blood bank policy was also intended as a simple solution to a problem thrown up by the bank's storage system, as all blood doned until this point had been labelled and filed alphabetically by surname rather than by blood group.

1977

Premium Bonds were officially launched by Hugh Gaitskell, the Emperor of the Exchequer, in his 1949 Budget. A monthly draw paid dividends to winning savers who chose to take part in what the Leader of the Opposite, Harold Wilson, dubbed *"this poshed-up version of a church bazaar raffle, sucking the last stinking pennies from the hungry purses of the flat-faced masses, I hate you, I hate you all"* before jumping from the visitors' gallery.

Despite this vicious attack, bonds were released onto an excited populace on Wednesday. Framley's first was legendarily sold by Mr Leonard Closed, proprietor of Closed Newsagents, to the lady mayoress at a brief ceremony in front of three children who were waiting to buy some cigarette chocolates.

The draws began in 1951 and a computerised mechanism was created - BERNIE (standing for *Bonds Equal Random Numbers I rEveal*) - which took over forty cautious years to select the first set of winning numbers. The backlog of weekly Premium Bonds draws (the results of the second are due in March 2033) meant that participants lost interest and drifted away and now other high risk gambling alternatives like the Notional Lottery are seen as much more viable ways of losing all your money.

WHAT WOULD YOU DO IF YOU WON £3?

CHECK YOUR BONDS

1985

Framley Zoo

Originally built in 1932 to house two foxes and the town's biggest hedgehog, **Framley Zoo** is one of the area's most popular touris attractions. But did you know that there's a history behind its famous bronze-plated gates?

From the gorilla protests of 1939 to 1982's experimental zookeeper breeding program, the zoo has always kept up with current trends and has been, I suppose, a mirror of society.

Today, it's still the number one choice for people who want to see what animals do in the wild when us humans aren't watching! But did you know there's a history behind Framley Zoo and its famous wooden gates?

In the late summer of 1979, Framley Zoo became home to an exciting new arrival - a **swiraffe**. Zookeepers and enthusiasts congratulated each other on five years' painkilling attempts to get a swan and a giraffe to mate.

The 15lbs female, christened Graham by the people who worked at the zoo, soon became Framley's most famous resident. Within weeks she was on TV (in the famous baked bean advert) and meeting Haircut 100 at the 1983 Annual Bravery awards.

Graham was even invited to Windsor Castle, but the zoo politely and controversially declined, fearing for the swiraffe's life at the hands of a maniac like the Prince of Edinburgh.

Sadly, by the end of that same year, everyone knew Graham's name. On the morning of 2nd September 1984, Graham was found to be missing, apparently stolen. Despite a huge publicity campaign and a dollop of national press coverage, she was never found.

And that's where the story ends. Graham turned up 48 hours later building a nest in the bins behind Freezo, and, clearly traumatised by the shock of being the victim of a thief, lived out her remaining days at a pet sanctuary on the outskirts of Europe.

The zoo was unable to recreate the breeding feet again, but is at the time of writing pouring millions of pounds into a project to cross a lobster with a pair of canaries, according to Gavin on the sausage stand.

1969

The biggest event of 1969 zoo-wise, was the donation of a **new lion** to the wil cats enclosure.

The lion, a gift from th animals at Peking Zoo, wa gratefully received althoug it was later discovered tha the keepers and authoritie at Peking had been unawar of the transfer.

As is traditional, loca schoolchildren were asked to name the animal, an out of the 3000 entrie there was one clear winne - "Paddington Bear"

Paddington Bear The Lio was intended as a mate fo Lemon The Lion, who ha resided at the zoo since 1963. The lif partnership of the two male lions caused outrage in th press and the Lord Chamberlain was forced to stick his oa in, decreeing *"this gay parade of jungle homosexuality"* illegal.

As a result, both animals were sentenced to be hanged a punishment for their "forbidden love". However, luc intervened when no volunteers could be found to try an hang them.

"Lions are dangerous when they're cross," one zoologis was reported as saying at the time.

OPPOSITE: A poster of the time advertising the popular "lion rides" fo children. The rides were less popular with the lions.

Ride the lions at Framley Zoo

Framley Zoo has three new lions - Daisy, Paddington Bear and Oggie - all waiting to give you a ride. Why not come down today?

Toys & games

We all have a favourite toy from our childhood, sometimes lovingly preserved into our adult years, sometimes thrown callously onto a bonfire in front of our streaming, red-rimmed eyes as we scream and scream and pound hopelessly on the unyielding legs of our father. On these pages we take a brief look at the Museum's collection of toys and novelties, many of which were generously donated by local people, or rescued personally by myself from bins and skips, searching, still searching, for Mr Wags.

BABY SPUD SPUD (1978)
Revolutionary at the time, a patented system allows the doll to produce mashed potato from its nose, ears and eyes, just like a real baby. A voicebox alerts the child to when the mash needs cleaning by declaring *"Mummy, I done spud-spud!"*. Flavour sachets were sold separately.

WHEELBARROW (1966)
The Game Of Opposites. A family prize puzzle from the makers of "Identity" and "ConnectiCones". Players compete to come up with an anwer to the question on the card, the game lasting until the question is satisfactorily answered. Each box contains a board, six tokens, one question and the FA Cup.

HAPPY FAMILIES (1886)
The well-loved card game, here s with the classic illustrations by Motown Brown. The aim of the ga is to try and collect sets of cards i "families" - husband, wife, son, daughter and best mate - without bursting into tears from boredom.

SMASHING CLOWN (1851)
An ingenious bedtime novelty from the Framley Toy Company, a cunning clockwork mechanism means the Smashing Clown can ride around a child's bedroom, systematically smashing all their toys with its tiny hammers while the child sleeps.

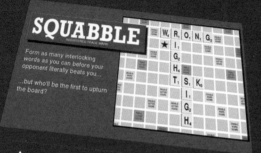

GOOSE FIGHT CARDS (1996)
Goose Fight had been a popular pastime in Framley for decades before the Newby Corporation thought of turning it into a collector's card game. The summer of 1996 saw playgrounds full of kids fighting over had the newest, rarest cards and smacking each other with socks full of coins until the Home Office poked their stupid noses in.

NODDING AUDIENCE (1958)
An endearing toy for the back shelf of the car. This row of appreciative plastic characters all applaud loudly when you reverse and agree fervently with your parking. Momentarily voguish in the late 50s, now usually sought after by retro-kitsch collectors or bakelite fetishists.

SQUABBLE (1986)
Squabble, "The *Can I Have A Word?* Game", has sold over a billion copies in the UK alone. The game is so popular that Squabble terms such as *"Go Away"* and *"Stupid Bloody Game"* have entered the English language where they now live.

SPELLING WASP (1882)
The explanation on the box of this Victorian educational toy reads as follows:
"This patented instructional novelty teaches a child to spell any word within ten minutes or you may claim from your supplier a free packet of replacement stings. Studies by the foremost medical and educational authorities have proven that the FINEST method of instruction for the younger mind is THREAT, and the WALDINGFORD LABEL-BRAND SPELLING WASP is assuredly THREAT enough, even for the most stubborn, recalcitrant or evil child. "I before E except after OUCH!" Not recommended for those of a fragile constitution or children."

MONOGAMY (1996)
Based on the popular stable relationship of the same name, Monogamy has been one of the world's most popular pastimes for almost a century.

ADVERTISEMENT

THE NAME'S BOMB... JAMES BOMB!*

Drive the OFFICIAL TR7 from the new James Bomb film, with its dazzling array of fully working gadgets!

Magnifying Glass (For looking for clues)

Roof-Mounted Spud Gun (Just like in the film!)

Knock-Down-Ginger Arm (Ring on the door of Viago's base... then drive away!)

Paper Shredder (with eight bits of official James Bomb paper to shred!)

Ian Ogilvy is Agent 7, James Bomb, licensed to spy, in 'Never Say Die', the latest Newby's Films production for Summer '83. And when James Bomb swings into action, he swings from the new TR7, packed to the tyres with eye-popping special features. As you can see, every one of those features is faithfully recreated in the Dunkie Toys model James Bomb TR7... Two lumps, not stirred!

🔲 **DUNKIE**   James Bomb Elite Cavalier Touring Caravan (with working Elsan toilet) available separately. (Not shown)

* The name "James Bomb" and the phrase "The name's Bomb, James Bomb" are not in any way connected to the trademarked character "James Bond" or any apparently similar copyright properties owned by the Eon Entertainment company. The James Bomb films are based on an entirely separate copyright property, "James Bomb's Home Handyman and Gardener's Guide", owned wholly by Newby Films Ltd.

1983

The Summer of 1983 sa[...] a totally new spy hero [...] take to the silver scree[...] and with him came all th[...] tie-in merchandise a spy could wish for, includi[...] this scale model die cast toy miniature car version of the full-size real non-toy car from th[...] blockbuster full-size film *Never Say Die*.

Sadly, this was to be thefirst and last time Sockford's Dunkie Toys would be able to manufacture a toy car related to the action adventure franchise. A multi-million pound lawsuit for infringement of intellectual prope[...] rights bankrupted fledgling production company Newby's Films within four days of the film's opening, and all prints of the film were impounded.

James Bomb will return in *Silvershot*.

1981

As the authoritie[...] had learned with[...] metrication and decimalisation, the key to introducing new ideas was to teach the next generation first before they in turn showed the last generation next - her[...] this lively ad campaign which ran in *Bangers & Mash* comic, using popula[...] television personality Dr Heinz Wolff (off *The Great Grape Race*).

What's the time, Professor Wolff?

Well, Jenny, that is quite a question...

Don't forget that from **June 6th** there will be **24 hours in every day**

60 minutes in an hour
60 seconds in a minute

The new times start on June 6th... Make sure you're up-to-clock

Trade your old watch in at your local jeweller's.

⬤ *THE BIG TIME CHANGE '8[...]*

DOCKING COMMENCE!

Meat Factory

Porridge (BBC TV)

Video Bingo

Goose Fight

Leyland Crisis

NBAA Baseball

THE NEXT GENERATION OF TELEVISION GAMERY IS NOW LANDING ON PLANET EARTH!

What's that coming over the horizon? It's the next generation of video technology for your home television! Lock your tractor beams on the jaw-dropping new **MOUTARDE SCREEN GENIE**™ from GEV...

So what's new? Well, the **MOUTARDE SCREEN GENIE**™ comes with a powerful 6K memory, twice as much as any competing TV game system, and eight times as much as your lawnmower. And that awesome power means faster response, more colours (eleven) and bigger joysticks for you to enjoy the **SCREEN GENIE**'s dozens of new games with!

And it's the games that make the difference. TV and film games, sports games, games with real cash prizes... There's even a game that does nothing at all, so you won't be distracted when the phone rings...

And the phone rings a lot when you've got a **SCREEN GENIE**™. Because once they know you've got one, everyone will want to play...

MOUTARDE SCREEN GENIE™

available from all branches of

NEWBY'S of Molford

1982

1985

CLASSIFIED SE

For ACTION ADS ring THE FRAMLEY EXAMINER on 0999 47694 U

① STUNTMEN

BOUND PARTWORK MAGAZINES. Fred Housego's Varnish Your Lounge magazine, with cassette tapes and ¾ tin of varnish. Tel Framley 75435

PEASE PUDDING HOT £12, Pease pudding cold £15, Pease pudding in ceramic presentation pot £20. Call 655784 (Advert 9 Days Old). Tel 0999 88290

ATHENA POSTER of a naked Ferrari Testarossa scratching its arse on a tennis court. Hideous. Absolutely hideous. £Hideous. Tel Codge 85109

STEVE JACKSON and Ian Livingstone's Fighting Fantasy Classified Ad Of Chaos. To buy an old wheelbarrow, call 0999 76454. To buy a tea crate full of sewing magazines, call 0999 95546. To attack the orc with your mace, call 0999 722187.

SOFT TOY orange cat with some sort of bog-eyed glandular condition and mild caffeine addiction. It's stuck to the outside of my window and it's looking at me. Make it go away. Offers. Sockford 52. Tel Chutney 6445

② TOM BOSLEY

RUBIK'S KALEIDOSCOPE. Try and arrange the coloured pieces in a non-symmetrical formation. Also solution book, "You Can't Do the Kaleidoscope" and pair of prescription contact lenses. £20. 890766

WEDDING DRESS. Ivory. 8' train. Veil. Peach edging. covered in assorted biological stains and chicken biriani. Call Mandy on Fram
66597 and mak

I DON'T KNOW where all these mice are coming from. Neither do you. But we will discover the answer together. Pamphlets - Fram 54767

FAN-ASSISTED Oven Gloves. My hands hot. Too, too hot. These gloves heap like oven. Call Little Cloud on Wripple 456

TOMMY COOKER'S Pressure Cooper. Produces 50 barrels a minute. 'Just Like This!' Whoft 65344

③ THE DARK DAYS

WALLETS! WALLETS! WALLETS! Credit cards, bank cards, organ donor cards. Visit Mr. Fry's Stolen Wallet Warehouse. Fram 78800

GEORGIA ON MY MIND. Professionally mounted . Will not separate. £80 Fram 63332

COMPLETE audio recordings of all of Michael Fish's television weather forecasts, collected onto cassette tape by holding the microphone up to the television speaker cone. Occasional interruptions by hoover and maternal dinner announcements. With display shelves. £130. Tel Fram 21060

STEELY DAN. Been up Walter and Boris Becker's arse a couple of times, hence £15. Buyer to retrieve. Framley 33881

RED-FRAMED SPECTACLES. Broken across bridge of nose. Result of unavoidable Mallett accident. Fram 72229

REMINGTON Victor Kiam. As annoying as the real Victor Kiam or your money back. Tel Marianne on 0999 39130

ECCLES SAPPHIRE caravan with fully working toilet, twin berths, gas stove and paintings of ballerinas being ticked th

"PROFESSOR BAFFLE" Electronic Game. Answers questions on maths, spelling and relationship issues using the voice of Bertrand Russell. Unnerving in every possible respect. Tel Framley 55287

④ RUBBER BABY

SPEEDBOAT. Cokefloat. Betablockers Buoy. Assorted maritime drug smuggling paraphernalia. Contact Farthings Wharf. Framley 0999 83727

BRIAN MAY signature telescope. Made from old mahogany fireplace. Refracting lens made from highly polished thruppenny bit. £700, that's why they call it Mr Farenheit. Tel Whoft 59902

ARE YOU a Whizz-kid or are you a Chip-ite? DNA testing kit. Fully certificated to British Medical Association standard. Sockford Pharmaceutical. 0999 44333

JOHN DELOREAN gull-wing trousers. Sides lift to display thighs...and more? Sockford 7632

TOURING CARAVAN Five years' experience in Jethro Tull roadcrew. Hard drinking, fast living, and riddled with gonorrhea. Qualified electrician and lighting engineer. £70 / day. Fram 46990

ABSOLUTELY EVERYTHING I've ever said. Printed onto 4" x 3" Flash Cards. Relive the magic! £7. Whoft 7773

SIMON BATES game. Electronic toy. Follow what Simon Bates says! Naggingly insistent. Hours of fun. £3. Wripple 1667.

PISS ARTIST'S EASEL props up the least rigid drinker

ZEISS 35mm Elitomatic Selective Lens. Removes unwanted subjects from your frame. Dull, unpopular people vanish from group photographs. Ideal for weddings. £17. 0999 74485

PENELOPE KEITH™ false teith. £5. 0999 36717

LASAGNE and chips. Two-thirds of a pint of IPA. 4 B&H. Phone now before Gary comes back from the toilets. Call Steve on 0999 46715

6 YEAR OLD child full of marbles. Call Mr Hollyhock on Framley 86619

I WILL burn all your money. Send all your money and I will send you a video of some fire. Discreet, essential service. Contact Vince on 0999 89191

WANTED. Dead or alive. Bronco Billy. For various public order offences including rustling, kidnap and being an ornery varmint. $250 reward. Apply Sheriff D'Ainty, Town Hall, Framley, quotin' reference "COWBOY DAY"

"STRETCH EDWARD HEATH" toy. Still in box. £ 0999 59950

⑤ SEX WITH HENS

FAT SUITS for fat people. real laugh riot. "The lif yours!". POA. Fram 4073

BOOK. Historic Fram Unwanted gift. Call Rowl on 0999 55352

BABY CARRIER. Top spe 25 Knots. Displaceme 19,000 tons. Two flight d and capacity for 14 babie hangars in hull. Of Framley 90662

ACUPUNCTURE needles have my doubts. Call between 8-10pm. Minu small cut, that's £300.

MOTH BOOKS almost plete set of "Best Left T Please. Just take them
73271

A Thousand Years of Stamps...

Framley Museum has been the lucky recipient of many extensive stamp collections, donated by local enthusiasts. Most notable amongst them was the **Walsingford bequest**, recognised by Scoffing & Fey Auctioneers to be the most valuable collection of stamps ever assembled in England. It is almost impossible to gauge the loss suffered by the world of philately at the hands of the freak tornado which swept through the Stamp Room within two days of the bequest being put on display. Thanks to generous contributions from visitors, however, the museum has begun to rebuild the collection, starting with these six stamps shown here.

ALFRED HITCHCOCK
GB, 1968
Commemorative

A striking stamp reversing the usual position of the royal silhouette and featuring the film director in a blink-and-you'll-miss-it cameo in the bottom right.

The Alfred Hitchcock stamp was issued in 1968 to commemorate the Master of Suspense's teasingly delayed twelfth birthday, just when we weren't expecting it - a mark of the Master's genius.

STAMP ON LOAN

"REARGUARD ACTION"
GB, 1983
Withdrawn 1983

This controversial 21p stamp caused quite a stir when it was issued in 1983. Sporting a saucy image of HM The Queen being taken roughly from behind by Captain Birdseye, the media were quick to condemn the Royal Mail for allowing such a stamp to see the light of day.

As any philatelist will tell you, no living commoner may be depicted on a stamp, and the breadcrumb-loving mariner had broken historic precedent. Of course, this stamp would barely raise an eyebrow these days (Captain Birdseye was made Duke of Edinburgh in the New Year's Honours, 1994).

POSTAL INSURANCE MICROSTAMP
GB, 1969
Abandoned 1971

This rare £23 microstamp is so small that a hundred of them would only be as wide as a human haircut.

Issued for insurance reasons, this tiny stamp needed to be licked and affixed to the top right corner of the enormous £600 stamp to ensure the high-value stamp reached its destination without being steamed off over the lunchbreak kettle by greedy postmen.

FLAVOURED STAMPS
GB, 1965
Discont'd 1967

...n innovative and highly ...ccessful idea, intended to get ...unger customers interested in ...nding letters, or just licking ...ngs, these clever stamps used ...voured glues to make them a ...icious alternative to dinner.

...'st released to mark 1965's ...ear Of The Sense", the stamps ...sted of whatever what was ...own on the non-adhesive side. ...e first selection depicted a ...awberry (1d), a pomegranate ...), a sandcastle (4d), a bald ...n opening a loft hatch (6d), ...e Duke of Argyll (1/-) and ...neone licking a stamp (1/6).

...dly the technique used was ...gotten in an industrial ...cident in 1967 and stamps ...erted to their default flavour ...boiled dead horse.

ZX79 SILICON STAMP
GB, 1980
Discont'd 1982

Far-sighted Framley technologist Peter Moutarde gave the country a revolutionary silicon chip stamp to mark the turn of the decade, and ushered in a new age of binary encoded philately that lasted nearly a year and a half.

More than just an adhesive square, cutting-edge microchip wiring meant that if you connected a pair of RS232 interface leads to either side of the stamp and plugged them into your kitchen light fitting, you could play a rudimentary computerised noughts and crosses game against your toaster.

A brief craze for stamp games followed. Nostalgic fans keen to relive their wasted youth will be delighted to learn that you can download an emulator program from www.petermoutarde.ac.uk that turns your Mac or PC into a stamp.

SILVER JUBILEE
GB, 1977
8p *Withdrawn*

Designers were in consultation for four years about the look of the stamp to mark HRH Queen Elizabeth the Second's 25 years of Silver Jubilees. According to consultancy panel leader The Very Reverend Darius Hawick, the process of selecting the image "did our bleeding heads in", but eventually the stamp above was unveiled on a first day cover on May 12th 1977.

The authorities withdrew the stamp almost immediately. Thankfully a letter to the General Post Office had alerted the authorities to their blunder: they had forgotten to put the Queen on.

Framley then and now...

The changing face of Framley is all around for us to see, if only we could go back in time and see how it used to be. And here's your chance!

1913 This view of Codge's Lambing Square shows the uneccessarily fussy 16th Century Community Arts Centre which was central to Codge's unparalleled development as a place of artistic excellence. The whole square was thankfully knocked down in 1995 and replaced with this wonderfully simple shack and a load of old trees. **1996**

1856 The temple ruins at Chutney provided archeologists with almost 150 years of fascinating study until, in 1988 Mayor William D'Ainty declared he was "fed up" with the site and sold it to a local property delevoper, on the condition that they build "some really funny houses". The corrugated tin box shown here was the first to be built and was opened by the giggling Mayor himself on the site of the old temple steps. **1994**

1860 Wistle, on the tributary of the River Fram near Urling, has changed unrecognisably in the past 133 years. Caught between two conflicting wind systems, most of the Garland-designed alms cottages are now up in the air, and, despite structural reinforcement, the ornately decorated Jacobean Guildhall is frequently found in Whoft. **1993**

4.11pm How the scene at the corner of Marsham Street and Williard Road has changed with the passage of time! That boy with the baseball has walked off and a lady with a bag has come round the corner. Surely it won't be long before the chemists closes - a sad sign of our difficult times. **4.14pm**

Framley then and now...

1920 / **1996**

This 1920 view of King's Mustard seen from the lens of Brian Wilson-Beard, Framley's tallest photographer shows the busy market town and its distinctive 12th Century cathedral, shortly before it was covered in snow. The heavy weather has still to lift, and the permafrost above the library is now 20 feet thick and Grade II listed.

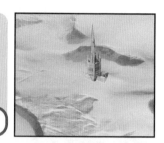

1900 / **1991**

How the coast at Clinton has changed over the 19th Century! To the farmers of 1900, the idea of a Channel Road must have seemed like a science fiction from the books of Jules Byrne, but 90 years later, traffic is speeding across the ocean. Though currently unfinished and awaiting permission to connect to a road somewhere in Europe, Framley's European Road Link remains a spectacular achievement.

1916 / **1995**

Pictured left, the mayor takes a salute during a wartime parade as it passes through the North End of Kidneyford. The harbour area was filled in with plywood boarding in 1979 to support a new access road for the toothpaste factory, and the Yacht Inn was pulled down and renamed the Bartholomew Tavern in 1985. The impressive Tudor buildings (right) were built in 1994, and are currently scheduled for demolition.

1904 / **1996**

The beautiful Pratcher's Cottage on the Molford Road has seen its share of changes through the passing years. In 1904, it was surrounded by fields and quiet lanes, overlooking the tranquil meanderings of the river Fram, untroubled but for the clip-clop of passing hooves. In 1996, however, it was on fire.

Framley now then, now then...

1928 Many traditional country crafts vanish in the face of progress. It doesn't seem so long ago that Chutney was the home to dozens of Mexican Road Dancers, and indeed, suburban streets and dual carriageways were still echoing to the sound of clopping feet and shrieking ladies at all hours of the day and night right up until 1968, when tetchy and sleepless residents volunteered Chutney as the ideal location for the Framley bypass. **1996**

1938 There have been some remarkable changes in the sleepy hamlet of Little Godley. A string of political upheavals in the tiny village have left their mark, with the humble cottages and winding lanes replaced by heroic architecture, tank-filled boulevards and monuments to the glory of far-sighted village ruler Councillor Haris Paris. The old forge (left) is now the state mausoleum of Mrs Paris who sadly died of snowball-related injuries in the winter of 1978. **1994**

1929 The Inman Inn in Inning-on-Ingbury was built in 1929 in a classic English rural style, and served the residents faithfully for 65 years, helping them get drunk and emotional. In 1994, grateful villagers presented the building with a beautiful carriage clock and the Inn retired to nearby coastal resort Onsey-on-Sea. The inn now spends its time relaxing on the beach and playing crazy golf with other old pubs. **1994**

1901 At the turd of the century, a few cows gather (left) in marshland beneath the shadow of the Bellaire Hillock. Innocent enough you might think, but within twenty years, these cows will have drained the marshland, built a network of dry stone walls and fences, developed opposable hooves and a rudimentary economic system and built The Freshborough Cow (right) visible for miles around. An ideal location for a picnic, if you don't mind being trampled angrily to death. **1996**

About the Museum

An overview by Leanne Digby-Bigdog, Director of Public Relations, Framley Museum

amley is a town with a long and fascinating history
d history, as Shakespeare said, is like a fishy on a
shy.

Elvis impersonator once admitted to me that
amley was the nearest town she'd ever been to.
aughed, because she had dreadful sunglasses. But
e also had a point. Framley is the nearest place to
y heart, because my heart is near Framley.

if it's the Victorians, the Georgian, the Belgians or
e bees you're interested in, Framley Museum is the
ace for you. With its many rooms full of fascinating
ings, there's someone for everything at Framley
useum.

ung or old, thick or thin, I'm sure you'll
st love Framley Museum. Even if
u've got no interest in history
hatsoever and don't care any
ots who invented the aeroplane

Don't forget to visit the cafe!

or the x-ray
deckchair or
whatever
Framley
Mueseum is the
place for you, but remember to stay
outside.

As Oscar Wild said, if you think
you're tall enough to try and see
the angels in heaven, make sure
you have someone shorter to look
out over up at with near by in case.

Or perhaps you'd like a nice
refreshing tea or a cup of ice-
cream? THEN GO TO THE CAFE.

WHEN DID YOU LAST SEE YOUR NAN?

e museum has dozens of interactive exhibits, and
nty that don't. Attendants will be onhand to help
, unless they are one of our non-interactive
endants.

t remember, the entire Framley Museum collection was washed away
floodwaters in 1981, so many of the exhibits currently on display have
en generously donated by local people from their lofts or collected from
storic car boot sales in the area. Maybe you can help.

e museum is free, but donations
£5 for adults and £3 for children
e compulsory.

odbye.

The award-winning Bee Wing, built in 1984, shows nature at
work in an exciting and accessible way. Over 1200 sq feet of
space is given over to a giant living hive, the entire wing full
to the brim with working bees. Access is via a steel ladder
and please do take care to close the door firmly on your way
in and out.

If you want to get even closer to nature, for a nominal donation
of £10, visitors can dress up as a bee and live as a drone for the
afternoon, although all pollen gathered must be returned to the
gift shop and any soiling of the costume or used stings must be
paid for. European safety guidelines force us to warn visitors
that using a sting can cause your buttocks to be torn off.

There's loads for kids to do too!
Why not visit the museum's
children's gallery's? There's no
end of push-button fun! Bench
grinders that play the speeches of
Neville Chamberlain and a
sandwich toaster to ride on, and
faece paints.

FRAMLEY MUSEUM
Learning from the past. Planning for the present
East Parkfields, Framley, FM1 8RD 01999 391 054

Kids' Kwest!

Fill in this fun questionnaire to find out if you've seen everything there is to see in the museum...

 Did you walk straight past the museum's boring collection of **flints**? ☐

Have you spent all of your pocket money on pencil sharpeners and fudge in the **Gift Shop** yet? ☐

 Did you build a working crab in the **God Gallery**? ☐

Did your parents tell you that you were adopted in the **Costume Gallery**? ☐

 Did you eat your Penguin bar and crisps and hide your egg sandwiches in a fishtank in the **Lunch Room**? ☐

Did you need to go to the toilet in the **Ceramics Collection**? ☐

 Did you see Alan Ridgwell being **sick** when he'd eaten too many aniseed balls? ☐

Have you tried encasing yourself in marzipan in the **Chamber of Cake**? ☐

 Have you felt how electricity works in the museum's **Fuse Cupboard?** ☐

Have you seen the **bearded** man in a scout uniform following you round the museum? *Call Framley CID on 01999 999 991* ☐

There's literally millions of fun things to do in Framley Museu For example this glass case full of Iron Age gynaecologi equipment and the stairwell.

 Can anybody smell **burning**? ☐

Did you make lots of **cobwebs** in the *There's No Turning Back Now, You're A Spider* exhibit? ☐

 Could you blow into this **bag** for me, sir? ☐

Did you try on Una Stubbs' underwear in the *Give Us A Clue* room? ☐

 Have you tried working for a tinpot little local newspaper for an absolute pittance whilst watching numbly as your **will to live** is slowly eroded? ☐

Do you promise to love, honour and obey the little girl filling in the **questionnaire** sitting opposite you, forsaking all others until death shall you part? ☐

If you've visited all of the rooms in the museum and answered all of the questions correctly then why not try doing it again dressed in a fox costume?

When We Were Pigs...*

If you've ever asked the question, "Which came first - the bacon or the egg?" then look no further than the answer! Because, in a quiet corner of the the grounds, between The Deadly Daffodil exhibit and the tribute to the Twenty-Three Policemen, sits one of Framley Museum's most popular exhibits.

When We Were Pigs is a fascinating re-construction of how life looked thousands of years ago... *when we were pigs*!

e When We Were Pigs exhibit was built for amley Museum in 1924 by local evolutionary eorist Chester White, and has proved popular er since. School parties welcome.

e statues in the exhibit have been verified as % accurate by the Chester White Institute, and e made of cement (not accurate).

ake cheques payable to The Chester White stitute to help our work promoting science in hools and colleges.

Human beings (that's us) share 99% of their DNA with pigs (they're them). You probably remember the nursery rhyme from your childhood:

C, G, T, C, A, G, T
A, C, G, A, A, C, T
G, C, C, C, T, G, A
That's why we're not pigs today!

Before they inhabited the wild plains and undergrow of Olde Englande, pigs (*hamo sapiens*) lived in the sea. Here they foraged for reeds and truffle clams, and made nests out of sponge. Their fat bellies and thick skins made them ideal for not swimming very well, and it is believed they soon started to drown and move on to the land.

The pig was an intelligent creature, able to adapt to any envoronment easily (except water). As these pictures prove, pigs invented the wheel, the horse, and (most importantly) tea. They lived in pagodas or one-sided houses, smoked pipes and ate salt, pepper and cake.

Archaeological digs have unearthed what may be religious relics, including busts, mosaics and primitive frying pans, suggesting that pigs worshipped bacon. Recent finds by the Chester White Institute have included a big piggy temple and the remains

of a statue of a dry-cured haunch surrounded by roast tomatoes.

But, no matter how faithful to their bacon gods these jolly pink animals may have been, their civilised lifestyle was not to last. In 410 A.D., pigs were all but wiped out when it rained people. Cascades of thousands of people falling hundreds of feet out of the sky crushed whole drifts of swine, reducing them to mere breakfasts.

However, the pigs that survived the deluge were taken under the wing of man, the new ruler of the world. He kept, bred, farmed, domesticated and ate his new friend, except some religious people who opted not to get involved in case the animals were dirty or god.

We know now that pigs pre-dated man by as little as several decades and as much as 11,000 years, thanks to some ideas found on a mountain range in China during the 1970s. Indeed, there is evidence to suggest that Jesus, Alexander the Great and Cleopatric Caesar were all pigs.

You can see all or some of this at **When We Were Pigs.**

*other theories are available.

Framley and district

Framley

Pop. 20,255 (1976). The first part of the name refers to the river Fram. The second means "shamble: or "upside-down horse."

The former Roman settlement of Frimulodonum, Framley was first mentioned in the Domesd: Book, where the *"uglye hamlet, Franley"* is recorded as a *"ditche or ponde."*

Once famous as the centre of the fluff industry, Framley is known world-wide today as the home Rawlinson's Awls, *"the finest way to make a hole there is.*™ *"* Framley is not a one-industry tow however, and a new industrial estate has opened on a brownsite site near Cossett Park.

Framley town centre is popular with shoppe

The church of St Dog-in-the-Manger's contains many fine 15th century architectural features, includir tweeves, archiblodes, mnesmenomes and flying fux.

Here Be Turnips was a 16th century coaching-house, in the yard of which was a mediaeval brew-shed from earlier inn on the site, The Big George.

Framley has good shopping facilities, with the modern **Arnhem Centre** its centrepiece. There is a large car pa at the rear of the 1960s' development in which many of the original graffiti survive. Early closing is frequent ar unpredictable.

Famous men whose names have been heard in the same sentence as the word "Framley" are reformer Gosne Evenmore, later Bishop of The British Empire, engineer Sir Bluff Furrow Gullimurph, and composer Alwy Tittershear, who wrote **HM The Queen**'s only single, *"Coronation Serenade,"* released in 1953, which wa number one in the hit parade for four and a half years.

Many M.P.'s from the town later became national figures, including Brian Furniture, Albit Mpeg and Dame Pol Wedgwood-Pott, who started as a humble secretary and went on to become Secretary to the Deputy Secretary the Home Secretary's Private Secretary.

Although Framley has some of the best sports facilities in this part of the country, its first brush with notorie was in 977, when **Bishop Dunroamin**, hanging from a rope tied to the town walls, asked everyone to wa beneath his feet as he kicked those he'd never liked in the hair. There are two swimming pools and a four ac crazy golf course with 837 holes.

Wripple

Pop. 1,976 (1976). "Silly upland".

A charming village of TV fame, lying beneath the Gloveswold downs. Cunnymede, the model village which depicts the entire village as it was in 1918 at twice its actual size, was built by Sir Constant Tiger in the grounds of his estate, Tiger Woods.

Codge

Pop. 500 (1976). "Cough; pandemonium."

Five miles N.W. of Durbiton. Darling House is posh, Plonkney's Farm and Sterling Mansion very posh, and Flutherhuther Towers, with its 3,000 peacocks, is not only astonishingly posh, but perilously dangerous.

Chipney

Pop. 840 (1976). "Field of potato."

Once the world's most prolific grower of potato, the land around Chipney is now completely potato-free, thanks to the Forestry Commission, which has reafforested the fields and streets with English Teak. Thereby, Chipney has given our language not only the word "Chip" but also the phrase "ploughshares into sideboards."

One of Wripple's lovliest corn

Bellaire

Pop. 460 (1976). "Fresh air."

Home of the Bellaire Hillock, which ha dominated the landscape since the nice age. Th mighty rock, which climbs over 200ft into the sk has never been conquered, despite attempts Lord Bile in 1902 and a team of Blue Peter pets 1977.

Princes Freshborough

Pop. 460 (1976). "Fresh breath."

Bellaire's next-door-neighbour, this village ar surrounding farmland was purchased by Josep Nitsy in 1828, and most of the houses date fro the Nitsy occupation. Nitsy's insistence that th houses should have no roofs or ceiling *"because only the Almighty and his elemen ought look down us,"* lasted almost a fortnight.

Batley

Pop. 3,280 (1976). "Battley".

One of Framley's most deprived suburbs, Batle is the most deprived suburb in England. Th name derives from Batley in England.

>flag THIS IS THE WRONG WAY UP KEITH:

The underground car park of St Kitten's, Glib

Clown

Pop. 0 (1976). "Mr Cellophane"

The forgotten village of Clown used to lie between Sockford and Whotten Plodney, until it wa swallowed by grass in the 1560s, following the levy of the disastrous Scythe Tax. By the turn of th 17th century, the village had completely disappeared under acres of overgrown lawn, an all to common occurrence at the time.

Glibley

Pop. 52 (1976). "That's easy for you to say."

Three miles north-east of the river Sock. Home of the famous Glibley point-to-point races, he every Easter Saturday, when young and old alike ride across the fields and hedgerows in pursuit chickens dressed as seasonal bunnies. The winner pulls the bird from its rabbit costume and mak it lay a chocolate egg.

Dungeon

Pop. 1,310 (1976). "Hill of bad shit."

Once an Indian burial ground, Dungeon has since been swallowed up by Framley's suburbs, and now the most crime-ridden estate in the world. Its unwieldy population, cramped into stinkir award-winning brutalist blocks of flats, comprises mainly loud-mouthed council-flat-bitch sing mothers with double buggies. It is also impossible to avoid crunched-up men resembling serious injured wolves, who should be avoided.

urbiton

op. 4,860 (1976). "Where ducks gather" or "Nice bingo lady's wobbly arms".

t Durbiton used to be found the headquarters of MMC, makers of Mixture Mate, the nation's favourite mixture. heir adverts famously boasted "a box and a half of mixture in every box of Mixture Mate." The town's principal mployer for over 70 years, Mixture Mate finally closed its doors and sacked its loyal workforce in 1989. Since en, the town has slowly started recovering, although many people still have trouble making mixture without eir loyal Mate.

hilillingbury Lillingbury lingbury On Ingbury

op. 850 (1976). "Ing's estate n the river Ill, by the L-shaped rn in the river Ill".

ngland's prettiest village. iloveswold-stone houses sing from a stream in a sylvan ombe, where pretty girls in ower-pattern dresses wave nd smile as they float past on ot buttered bicycles, and hot weet tea is served with hot weet cream horns covered in :ing sugar and sauced in hot weet honey. Not for the faint f tooth!

hoxtoxeter

op. 260 (1976). "Thoxton's oisonous-smelling farm".

he five almshouses in the ain village street are known ocally as "The Fingers". The oet Owen Eyebrow wrote *"My ife As A Cauliflower"* at Index ouse, and both Little House nd The Thumb are said to be aunted or sticky.

Mr. Mixtures

So Mr. Mixtures, what's the good of making a meal without any Mixture Mate in it?

"Well, for a start you'd never get that flavour that your family expect from their food. You wouldn't get that authentic *freshly laid* smell. There'd be nothing to drink with your meal."

"And after you've eaten, how would you clean the plates? Or, for that matter, dry them again afterwards? You'd have nothing to eat the meal on, or to wipe yourself with after a *little accident*."

Next time you're considering cooking a meal without Mixture Mate, just think about what you've just been told and what you'd be leaving out.

It's almost impossible to comprehend.

Don't forget the mixture... Mixture Mate!

ffing Sodbury

op. 880 (1976). "Peat house, nsuitable for children."

ome of the famous Effing odbury carnival, held annually. Fire-eating pantomime horses race each other around a crazy- ouse shooting coconuts full of goldfish, while a parade of wicker cheerleaders tight-rope-walks cross a giant teacup, and steam engines driven by tigers run amok through the crowds. wondrous local spectacle *(not pictured)*.

venly

op. 355 (1976). "Certainement il fait chaud aujourd'hui".

nlike its soundalike, Slovenly, Ovenly is heavenly. The church of St Sharpener has a beautiful turistic chancel arch, and contains the 16th century tomb of Ludby Chantrey Chappell in a lovely antry chapel.

St Eyot's and district

St Eyot's Castle is one of the best preserved exa

St Eyot's

Pop. 5,266 (1976). "Church of St Eyot".

St Eyot (pronounced "Eight") founded the monastery at Deyaughthcan's Chine (pronounced "Chine") in AD320 and gave his name to the town that now bears his name. The town formed part of the Glansby estate until the 1600s when it was given to a man in a pub by the then Earl of Glansby in exchange for a spectacular pair of shoes that the next morning turned out to be a design on the pub flooring. The famous 14th Century castle is one of the most complete examples of late Norman showing-off in the region.

Slovenly

Pop. 1,116 (1976)   "G of Dorset, inheritance is hidden behind dressing table"

Birthplace of Framley's ebullient mayor, William D'Ainty. The beautiful 12th Century Priory at Ogden's Mount mentioned in Thackeray and also in the middle eight of *Three Is The Magic Number* by De La Soul. Slovenly ha a vibrant harbour district that attracts tourists and crabs. The elaborate medieval cobblestone high street wa built by midgets captured in the crusades.

Urling

Pop. 408 (1976)   "Garden full of old lawnmowers"

Nestling in the arm of the river Fram, Urling is home to the Urling Grandfathers, Britain's smallest football tean The seventeenth century pond was built on the site of a sixteenth century pond and was the first in the region t be treated with duck-resistant artex.

The church at Urling contains relics from the 1976 FA Cup final

Fracton

Pop. 1,893 (1976) "Settlement behind enormous ditch"

Genteel Fracton sits in stark contrast to its gaudy neighbou Clinton. Its inhabitants resist change, and its Regenc seafront is refreshingly untouched and closed to nor residents. Fracton was used as the location for the cult 196C TV series *The Enigmatist* and fans gather every year i Clinton to squint wistfully up the FR411 in the vague directio of the exclusive resort town.

Clinton

Pop. 3,609 (1976)   (origin obscure) "Clyn's ballbearinç thankyou grape mountain" or "Clyn's settlement"

Originally a tithed smallholding to the Rumphall Estate Clinton expanded dramatically in the 1800s with the comin of the railways and the vogue for gaiety bathing. The pier an pleasure gardens were completed in 1896, with characterist pornographic ironwork by Sir Daniel Factfinder. The dome ceiling of the pier head ballroom is visible from space but nc visible from the pier itself, a trick of the light that has led t the pier being adopted as the international calibratio standard for orbital survey telescopes. There are four time as many fruit machines in Clinton as there are anywhere els

Mapton Nogley

pop. 315 (1976). "Nuaga's farmstead in a terrible bother".

Mapton Nogley old town is now almost entirely deserted, the erection of the GEV Telecom Mast on the village green in 1998 having driven out any residents with strong views on brain cancer. House prices in neighbouring Mapton Nogley Carnival Village however remain popular. The sports centre was opened in 1981 by Suggs and features Britain's only indoor waterskiing pool.

Stanglebridge

pop. 85 (1976). "St Anne's disappointing holiday"

Once the home of St Anne's Dye Works. The dyemakers here popularised the colour orange in the early nineteenth century, eventually influencing plant breeders to develop the tie-in fruit. When the factory closed in 1936, the town was given back to the flood plain, after long negotiation between representatives of both the dye works and the river.

One of the least annoying parts of Stanglebridge.

Yopney St Oh!

pop. 92 (1976). "Yapp's meadow by the river sacred to St... I've fallen in"

A picturesque hamlet on the main Roman road out of Framley, Yopney has always had great strategic value for anyone wishing to attack the town. In 1943, British Intelligence discovered that the village had been entirely populated by German spies in deep cover since August 1918. Yopney is also a favourite stop off point for birdwatchers keen to see the last breeding pair of Gold-Hooped Rabbit Buzzards in captivity, in the family room of the Bear and Cretin pub. Please keep children's hands inside the pushchair.

Queff

pop. 284 (1976). "Dirty boy"

The village name derives from the Old English word *Cwéad* meaning mud or dirt and refers to the mud which fills the streets to calf height for most of the year while the river Fram is in high flow. George Mousehat wrote *Nanderby Chase* while trapped in a barn here, transcribing the entire novel in longhand onto all the paper he could find in his pockets before realising the door opened inwards.

Gartside Green

pop 147 (1976). "Smooth patch of grass (by the) smoother patch of grass".

Some of the Gartside Fusiliers who acquitted themselves so nobly at Rourke's Drift that they were preserved in bronze in Framley Regimental Museum, killing them. The remains of an early motte-and-bailey castle can be tasted in the shepherd's pie at the Gartside Lounge. The church of St Anne-Le-Knife is said to be haunted by the ghost of a pair of trousers left by a bridegroom in 1911.

Molford and district

Molford

Pop. 8,401 (1976). "Shallow crossing point of river, filled with dead moles".

A modern suburb, 3 miles in any direction away from Framley. Molford was revitalised in the 20th Century by th arrival of Roy Newby, and his octopoid Rakes and Essentials shopping empire. After decades of heate negotiation, all retail outlets in the town are now owned by the Newby corporation, and the pound is no longe legal tender (having long since been replaced by Newbytokens each worth £1). Molford is also also the offici birthplace of Mayor William D'Ainty al Molfordi. D'Ainty's actual birthplace, Slovenly, celebrates his birthday c a different day of the year, in accordance with royal precedent.

The Kentucky Fried Chicken Drive Thru in Molford St Gavin

Molford St Gavin

Pop. 698 (1976). "St Gavin's drowning of the moles"

Simply dripping with cash but known locally as a particular sensitive village, Molford St Gavin's main feature is St Gavin Chapel. Built of flints, pudding stone and hamster teeth, th church has an unnaturally gaudy 15th-century tower carrying peal of bells. None of the three bells are inscribed. All three a replacements made from parachute silk, installed after th original bells were taken away to be melted down to make be for the war effort.

Molford St Malcolm

Pop. 1,264 (1976). "St Malcolm's artificial respiration of the mole

By a curious geographic quirk, Molford St Malcolm is actual closer to the moon than it is anywhere else. In the 13th centu permission was granted for an official weekly market in Molfor St Malcolm and the ancestors of the original stallholders are st trying to sell exactly the same goods today.

Houseboats and Domestic Submarines crowd along t

Molford St Arahim Rhamal

Pop. 1,962 (1976). "Non-permanent member of the UN Security Council"

Weather managed to cause disruption in 1833 with gusts of up to 100 mph uprooting a windmill. The sails spun at such a rate that the mill tunnelled through the earth's crust and soon reached Brisbane, leaving Molford St Arahim Rhamal with a literal tourist trap, the Antipodean Chute. For a small fee, Victorian danger seekers could visit the other side of the planet on a fire-resistant bungee rope in less than 15 seconds. A bronze engraving of a man in a deerstalker emerging from the ground in front of confused Aborigines, feet first and at great speed, is on display in the Framley Museum.

Robot Oak

Pop. 39 (1976). "Deciduous aluminium; a boogie-boogie acorn"

An inorganic hamlet situated at the gateway to Iffing Forest, developed as an experiment in utopian living in the early and all of the 1970s. No natural materials whatsoever are used in Robot Oak. Polyester hedges divide nylon allotments where acrylic fruit and vegetables are grown to feed the steady population of thirty-nine cellulose automatons, who keep themselves largely to themselves. Home to the largest municipal dump in the Northern hemisphere, the sky above which contains an average of 75.1 seagulls to every square foot.

Ghastley St Matthew

Pop. 558 (1976). "Minnie Riperton once slept here"

Formerly known as Absolutely Grotesquely St Matthew, the village changed its name after the old church was bulldozed and replaced with a marginally more pleasant looking one. Home to The Old Barn which runs both sides of The Old Barn Street. The barn once housed the largest brood of gala pie-egg producing hens in the world until animal rights activists released them in 1987. The fowl were left free to roam the streets where they now lay terrifying quantities of free-range eggs measuring anything up to a furlong in length. A local industry manufacturing long spoons and stabilized eggcups flourished briefly in the late 1980s although it collapsed soon after, as the employees were too busy trying to finish their breakfasts.

Crème

Pop. 202 (1976). "Pleasure, but not necessarily for pleasure's sake".

The name is pre-English. Once a haven for peasant thrift, the wars with Little Godley and the influence of wealthy landowners have made Crème a place of commercial thrift. Pre-decimal currency - including groats and denarii - are still accepted in the delightful Post Office, where penny chews remain ten-a-penny. The mediaeval church of St Dragon's has an authentic Norman kitchen which still employs a Norman cook.

A homeowner receives her test results in Crème

Tollephant

Pop. 397 (1976). "Many a muckle makes a mackleackleackle"

Almost entirely parkland, Tollephant is home of the wettest park bench in Britain, adorned with a plaque which reads, *"In loving memory of Arnold Flower, 1889-1967: he loved this place. It may have given him an arsehole like the Japanese flag but he still loved it anyway".*

Peaceful riverside at Strawbury Magma

Strawbury Magma

Pop. 149 (1976). "Hot purée within crust of village"

Once a major Saxon settlement, picturesque Strawbury Magma now regrets the parish council's 1932 decision to employ the renowned artichect Sir Brian Clough Ellis-Bextor, a self-made alcoholic and recovering millionaire to modernise the village. After his plans for a redesign of the main thoroughfare were approved and built to his exact specifications, Sir Brian stalked the streets with a bullwhip, grievously injuring anyone not standing in the exact pose and location of the tiny figures in his original scale model.

Diesel Park West

Pop. 4 (1987) "Dylla's farmland in the West"

The village of Diesel Park West released its first album in 1989, having signed to Food Records, home of Jesus Jones and Blur. Though the village encountered some commercial success through the support of parent label EMI, a breakthrough eluded it and the sleepy hamlet retreated from studio and live work, eventually resurfacing on a series of smaller labels in the mid 1990s.

Sockford and district

The only surviving Sockford Squab, a prototype wheel-less one-seater, ta[...] pride of place as the centrepiece of the the Museum's car garden, whic[...] deemed an area of special scientific interest, so we never mo[...]

Sockford

Pop. 2,680 (1976). "Ford by the river Sock".

One of the fastest growing towns in the area, Sockford was originally a smallholding. By the late 1900s, it h[...] become a bigholding, and was home to many light industries such as Tomskworth Gas Lights and Possibly Fittin[...]

The coming of the motor-car meant the motor-car arriving in Sockford, when, in 1922, the Associated Motor Wor[...] opened. The twelve-acre plant mass manufactured the Model One and the Bitmap MkVII.

By the time of the Second World War II, over 800 people worked at Associated. The plant was adapted [...] manufacture munitions and tin shoes during wartime, but returned to carp roduction in the early 1950s, turni[...] out over 2 million of their best-selling model, the Operator.

Associated Motor Works grew with the success of the Operator, and by 1971 had over 8,600 employees. Desp[...] rocky times during the 1980s, when they faced competition from the new Apollo Creed 4 Series, the plant is s[...] productive today.

The last Operator rolled off the production line in 1976, and is buried in the churchyard at St Wednesday's.

Lessbury Moreborough

Pop. 511 (1976). "Large Village" or "Small Village".

Following the Poor Law of 1836, picturescue Lessbury was chosen as the site of the new Sockford District Workhouse. Overseen by social reformer Sir Malcolm Bunglebonce, the home cared for the tramps and "casuals" who passed through the town. After a hot meal and bed, the staff would send tramps off the next morning with clean ears and a purse containing £11,000 for the journey. The Workhouse closed in 1837.

Sockford attracts art lovers keen to visit the streets that inspired local artist Ibrahim Bethsheveth to move elsewhere.

Whoft and district

Whoft

Pop. 8,440 (1976). "Silent but violent."

Whoft lies in the centre of the region and was once the county town before Framley was discovered to be 1/16th more attractive and thus more likely to be featured on the *Antiques Roadshow*. The area's history can be traced back to before prehistoric times; a mammoth penis is proudly displayed in the foyer of the library on the first Tuesday of every month. Two Whoft men, Abel and Babel Luscombe sailed on the Mayflower to the New World in the 17th Century but got mashed by sharks whilst attempting to invent water-skiing. There is also a miniature railway running through woodlands which is great for families although not so great for wildlife.

Whoft is currently in the process of reconstruction, after a planning blunder in 2002 destroyed the whole town. Sights used to include the then-intact ancient seven-sided cross which was by what used to be the river, near the since-pulverised church where a heap of rubble now stands.

It also used to be possible to enjoy the 16th century tanning salon and nearby Happy House, with its famous bass line. The site is now given over to builders' portacabins, and looks a bloody mess.

Rotten Plodney

Pop. 710 (1976). "You are leaning against an open door, sonny." Variously recorded as "Rotten Rodney," "Whatter Plonkney" and "Vombling Wembley."

Home to the world-famous Puddles brewery, winner of the Rotten Plodney only employer of the month award for six years running. Other places to visit include the Georgian mansion, Hesslaw Halt. This dilapidated property was landscaped by Cacophony Taupe and has subsequently been disowned by English Heritage. A light skirmish on the outskirts of the town in 1939 finally escalated into the Boer War several hundred years later when the ancestors of the instigators were sent to Boerland.

Queues Likely

Pop. 772 (1976). "Of, for, or relating to the nose."

The Black Death was launched in 14th Century Queues Likely and became so widespread that 127% of the villagers perished from the disease. The negative number of villagers had huge families over the following years in an attempt to repopulate and by 1398 the population numbered -571 until they were all turned inside out by order of the King and the problem solved. Lord Nelson is touted to have frequently stayed at The Roach & Horse Inn with his lover, Mr Hardy, where the landlord was perfectly happy to turn a blind eye to that sort of thing so long as he could watch.

Right Angle Cottage, Whotten Plodney

Little Godley

Pop. 828 (1976). "Crafted from the thighs of tiny giants."

The Foreign Office has advised all British nationals to avoid Little Godley due to the prospect of civil unrest in the area since Councillor Haris Paris's military coup in 1994. The Witchradar General, Nightnight Hopkins, once sat in judgement on women thought to be witches at the Crown Inn. His verdict would be announced at the end of an all day session, generally "Grffffthmp" as he slumped into a plate of cold meat and boiled potatoes. 512 suspected sorceresses were burned at the stake until Hopkins died in 1967.

Chutney

Pop. 2,639 (1976). "The Best of Roger Whittaker".

Until the 17th century, Chutney was home to a population of indigenous mermaids. The villagers lived in civilised harmony, combing their hair and seducing sailors. Then, in 1685, they were completely wiped out in the famous Chutney Clearances. A group of hunters and thrillseekers arrived in skiffs and culled the fish. Their oily bodies were made into soup, and their scales into gloves. Glovemaking thrived in the town until the 1920.

One of Chutney's biggest claims to fame is as the ancestral home of two former presidents of the USA - Richard Nixon and J. Danforth Quayle. The parish church contains a reredos displaying the Quayle family's coat of arms with their motto, *"Ich bin ein potatoe"*. The church greets you as you approach the town centre; local opinion is divided as to how and why the church does this.

King's Mustard

Pop. 68 (1976). "If this is Mustard then I'll be an uncle's monkey".

The vertical main street is a rarity in the county, and was recently awarded a lottery grant due to its 1:0 gradient. Abseiling equipment has been provided and a temporary lift installed, although the oxygen tanks needed to visit Shandy's Chemists of 68 Tall Street have recently run out.

The parish church of St Maplin's in Steeplecocqueboasts an olympic-sized ◼

Without Sir John Battleship's revolutionary sewage system of 1881, this view down Chutney High treet would have been entirely obscured by dung.

Clifton James

Pop. 145 (1976). "(Some kind of) doomsday machine".

The fine, sweet Gloveswold turf was made by nature to the home of sheep: champion sheep that yield rich Clift James mutton. Champion sheep that compete with oth champions at the country show, being carefully groome along with all the other champions. Where, in a holid atmosphere, the country and the town get together: farm and statesman meet over a pint of mildly drinkable.

Pity, then, that no sheep have ever been reared in Clift James, and that no such country show exists he Sometimes it is a lonely planet.

Steeplecocque

Pop. 109 (1976). "Chicken-like tower structure".

Once the seat of the Steeplecocques, influential landowne and fraudsters, the area is now very different kettle of peop

At Pancake Rectory, the Rev Albert Prickles was bo whose diaries record his father's weekly target practise his benighted son. Prickles was made to stand in a she while his strict Presbyterian father fired boiling apples him, inspiring his later memoir, *"On Being The Target O Madman With An Armful Of Hot Fruit"*.

Outlying districts

arnaby Constable

op. 54 (1976). *"Green Dock".*

nis tiny village is noteworthy for two reasons; its church's
nusual altarpiece - a giant wooden bear eating Whoft
urch - and being the birthplace of the C16th architect
verage Po. There are numerous examples of Po's work
) be found on display, such as the *Raven House* in the
iddle of the village green and the post office's ornate
ountain Go-Round.

loxted

op. 5 (1976). *"Where the Oak Trees roam".*

ossibly the smallest village in the area, Cloxted isn't
ally much to talk about. There's a house, a farm and
at's it. In fact, I'm not even sure the house is there
nymore. It's got a nice sign.

ockney

op. 157 (1976). *"Place of the pub and the rock".*

ust after leaving Purge on your way east out of Framley,
ou pass through Rockney. This village is home of the
mous *Humpty Horse* public house and in turn the
rthplace of *Eggstone's Batter Bitter* with its distinctive
aming bottom.

The famous pier at Hazeldean Inchmistress

market square at Billberry Buryborry still looks similar to itself.

Hazeldean Inchmistress

Pop. 975 (1976). *"Hazeldean Inchmistress".*

Coastal town. Hans Christian Andersen famously spent
5 nights at Hazeldean Inchmistress' fire station and it
was here that he wrote *Charles Dickens.*

Billberry Buryborry

Pop. 4872 (1976). *"Berry and Bile Heap".*

At the centre of the high street in this quaint town still
stands the original *Berry Spinner's Arch,* where market
traders would hang their berries to ripen before
spinning to market. The berries found in the locality are
highly poisonous and would have been sold as a novelty.

Nyth

Pop. 320 (1976). *"Too Near"*

There is evidence of early settlement at Nyth dating
back to the Iron Age. Extensive Roman remains,
including a beautifully preserved Roman archaologist,
were found during construction of the A999 in 1986, as
well as a fine example of a medieval wristwatch.

FRAMLEY AND DISTRICT
ARCHAEOLOGICAL & LOCAL HISTORY SOCIETY

William Blenheim-Punt, Chairman of the Framley and District Archaeological & Local History Society (pictur at Sockford Beefeater Reserve (above left (right)), the Chutney Dyche (above centre (left)) and lost (above rig (third left)), helping other members to enjoy days out that he organised himself, all of which were very successf

The society, founded in 1981, exists to encourage research into the history of the local area that might uncov anything less predictable than our existing members have managed thus far. Membership is open to all wi an interest, particularly if it is in local history*.

Although the society was recently relegated from Division 12 of the Local History Society League, we have ju been informed of our possible reinstatement pending an investigation into irregularities in the publishe findings of the Molford Antiquarians. It appears that only 16% of the excavated bones are currently account for. Clumsy old Clive.

Unless your name is Rathbone Twiddrington or Oswald Underclown. Where did you bury all of our spades?

Over the summer the society is planning visits to various local places of interest, including the Fluff Mill at Framley, the site of the former Tesco supermarket next to the bypass and the old woman who used to be a shoe.

The trip to the brewery at Whotten Plodney will be followed by a brief but decisive skirmish with the Molford Antiquarians before boarding the coach. Members old and new are invited to bring a broken bottle and a picnic lunch.

It's never quite as much fun when it's cold and wet so during the winter months we hold a series of lectures that reflect this.

Tuesday, 12th November
"Looking Back At Pastures New"
- Mrs Margaret Helpful

Tuesday, 26th November
"Coin Or Amphora: The Beginner"
- Derek Archer

Tuesday, 10th December
"They Lived Very Happily Together"
- Mrs Margaret Helpful

Tuesday, 24th December
"A Neolithic Christmas Pantomime"
- Mrs Margaret Helpful

All lectures start at 8pm prompt

Contact:
W. Blenheim-Punt
1 The Maltings
Wripple End
FR6 3FG
E-mail:blenheimpur
@1themaltings.co

Page designed by W.Blenheim-Punt on a Gateway personal computer © 2002

For the last three years, Chairman of the Framley and District Archaeological & Local History Society, Willia Blenheim-Punt, has put his name forward to receive an MBE in recognition of all the work promoting histo in Framley that he has encouraged and watched. Please contact the Chairman if you can help in any way.

Framley Film Society

The Cat Stevens Lecture Pyramid, Framley Community College, Froth Street, Framley FM1 3TB

LIST OF VIDEOS HELD IN THE COLLEGE ARCHIVE

Note - these are only available for viewing on the premises, tapes must not be taken away and have Ground Force taped over them, Martin

ELLAIRE	- *To Bellaire by Barge.* 4 year land-locked journey. 1954.
LINTON	- *Tuppenny Toss Off.* Dockside life in 1950s Clinton.
ODGE	- *A Reflex Spasm in the Stomach.* Codge Meals-on-Wheels. 1972.
RAMLEY	- *Get Back in the Barrel.* Child care in the 1950s.
RAMLEY	- *What I Did On My Bestest Weekend.* Two days in the life of the Bishop of Framley. 1901.
RAMLEY	- *Framley On Film.* How a Public Records Film is Made. 1963.
RAMLEY	- *Operation Dungdrop.* Film diary of the Mayor of Baden-Schleissgarten's aerial visit to Framley in 1978.
RAMLEY	- *Shhhh!* The Framley Youth Orchestra, 1965.
RAMLEY	- *AC-3CCTV270587.*The Arnhem Centre. Security Camera 3B, Wednesday 27/5/87.
RAMLEY	- *Betrayed!* VE Day in Framley. 1945.
RAMLEY	- *Framley On Fire.* An arsonist's account. 1959.
RAMLEY	- *Heaven Can Wait.* The 1968 Vicar Strike.
RAMLEY	- *Mince Matters.* The phasing out of free school mince in 1973.
RAMLEY	- *Rubbish Rubbish.* A year in the life of a tin can at Framley Municipal Dump. 1983.
RAMLEY	- *Did We Take Sugar?* The mental stability of Framley Mental Health Service. 1986.
RAMLEY	- *Does France Exist?* Council debate on proposed rail link to channel tunnel rail link, 1994.
OLFORD	- *Wripple is Shit.* Molford Film Club. 1991.
OLFORD	- *Dr Who. The Dalek Master Plan* (12) The Destruction of Time tx 29.1.66
OLFORD	- *Playing With Balls.* Rapidly deteriorating footage of the 1997 Gregory's Girl's School 6th-Form Volleyball tour.
OCKFORD	- *When Louis Met Jimmy.* Louis Armstrong & Jimmy Schlongle Durante at the Sockford Polyhedron, 1941.
OCKFORD	- *Approaching Midday.* A year in the life of a minute - all the 11:59s from 1968.
OCKFORD	- *Willow & Giles Do Sockford.* Buffy fan fiction, Sockford Amateur Dramatic Society. 2001.
EYOT'S	- *Building for the Future.* 1938 film of the construction of the 852acre Delling Housing Estate for tortoiseshell cats.
EYOT'S	- *Straight Down the Line.* The St Eyot's Cartographic Society's mapping of the horizon. 1962.
HOFT	- *Full Circle.* A Whoft wheelwright's year and suicide. 1954.
HOFT	- *A Nowhere Near Brief Enough History of Drainage Equipment.* A lively look at the history of drainage equipment in the area. 1992.
HOFT	- *Ground Force 15/4/98.* With 2 minutes of very rare footage of construction of Whoft Reach railway station at either end.
HOTTEN PLODNEY	- *A Box o' Crabs.* Folk singing in Whotten Plodney marketplace, 1932.
RIPPLE	- *Wicker Basket Making.* Red Hot Dutch action. 1976.
RIPPLE	- *The Dance of the Dots.* Wripple Diceworks. A film record from 1937.

Index

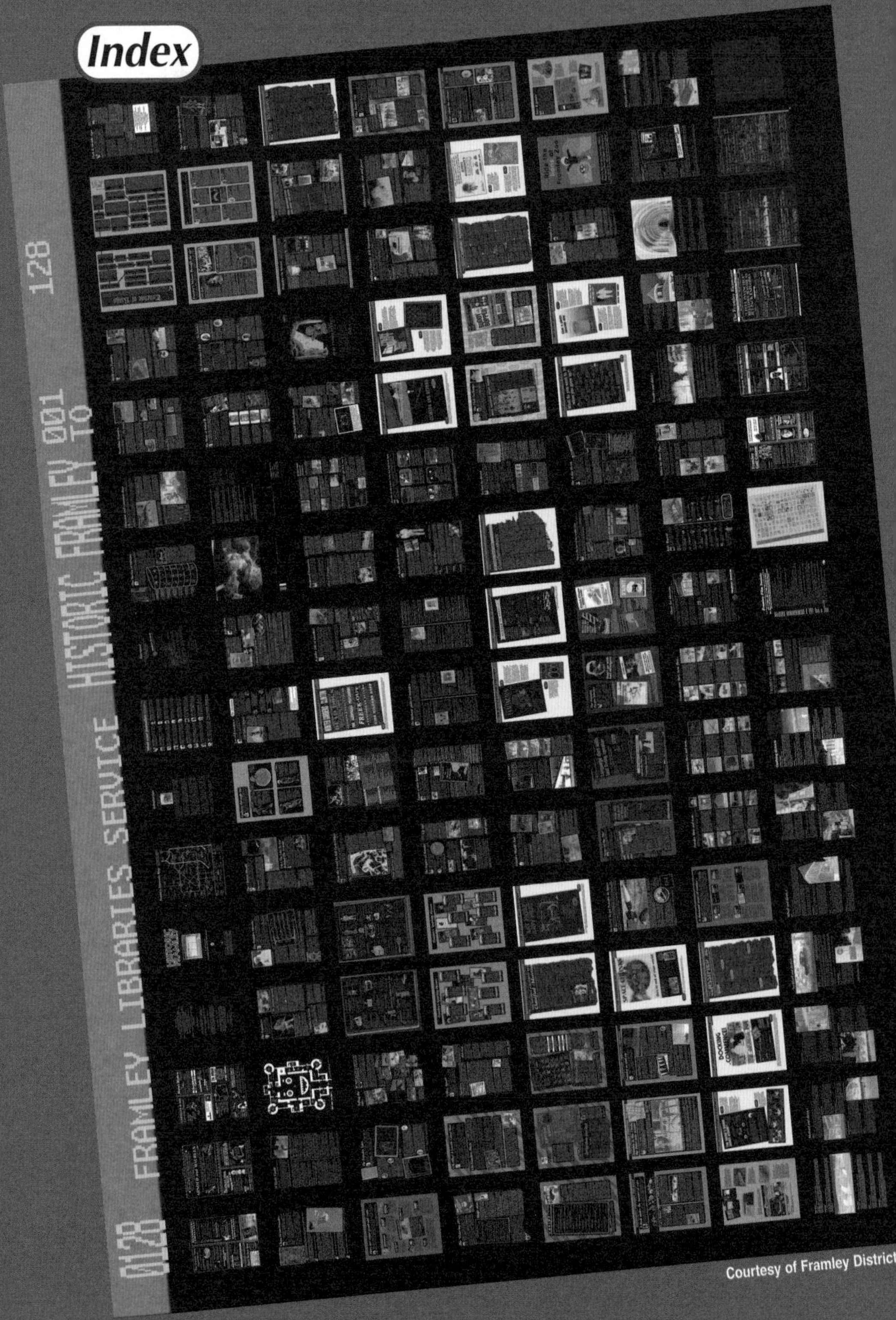

Courtesy of Framley District

CARDIGAN & SON
Canoeing Funerals

"It's what he might have wanted"

- Blade McAllister
Sockford Chapter
Hell's Kayaks

Full sendoff with dignity and a cagoule.

Choice of traditional burial, or the body of your loved one delivered into the mercy of the flames in a low brace roll.

CARDIGAN & SON
109 Michigan & Smiley Road,
Ghastley St Matthew, Framley
01999 76 76 90

Discretion, courtesy, canoes

Hotel Hydro

£12.99

15-32 Blegvad Avenue, Chutney.
01999 648479
www.chutneyleisure.com/watersports.html

SWIM LUNCH OFFER!!!!!!!!!!
3-course meal followed immediately by extensive water leisure facilities and easy transport links to Framley General Hospital afterwards.

Sockford ෯ Cycles

Sockford's biggest selection of one- and three-wheeled bikes!

SORRY! 2 sold out!

Saloon and Hatchbikes
Stupid helmets

JUST IN!

Yamaha 6-String Racing Bike

73, Mechanical Idiot Avenue,
Sockford (opposite Golley's)

Tel: 01999 592212
Fax: 01999 592213
Bike: 41-65 00 (ext 771)
Teleport: A3- 14'3"N, 11-44

P.E.KITT

Licence Architect
Whoft 8677
Mobile: Orange
or email us for
instant building

---

24 HOUR
PLUMBING SERVICE

Flushing a toilet? Emptying a washing up bowl? Putting a plug on the end of a chain? Hiding a tap under your pillow?

Even if you only want a new washer on a tap, I GUARANTEE it will take me 24 hours.

NO JOB TOO BIG!*
01999 542542

(*unless it's bigger than these jobs)

NEW FROM TAIWAN
JUST 18
VIP Bubble Bath Service

otel / B&B
sits   Body to Body

UXURY SURROUNDS

1999 235576
ALL ME!
MAKE ME SHOUT

SINGLES ONLY
GLASSBLOWING NIGHTS

Fascinating Pastime! We will blow you a wife/husband/? as you watch. Remember glass partners are easier to clean and shut up.

Durbiton Glass Works, 3 Grande Marchee, Durbiton FM7
www.durbitonglass.co.uk   email: info@durbitonglass.co.uk

Dungeon Working Men's Club

What's on at the DWMC? Weekly entertainment at Dungeon's finest!

MONDAY MONDAY MONDAY

Quiz night

Rotating themes every week of the month.
Call Tony for more details.

WEEK 1 - Sport
WEEK 2 - Pop & Music
WEEK 3 - The Fall of Troy
WEEK 4 - The Life and Novels of Franz Schubert 1978-86

Bonus points for Lumpy Dick round.

£1 entry per person. Tony's decision is usually final.

TUESDAY TUESDAY TUESDAY

Two Ffat Lladies Lltd present
Welsh Tribute Bingo

Llegs LL!

On its Owen, number 6

2 Llytl Dwchs, 22

Llylity Llyll - 66!

Top prize £111!

You Swnch My Battleship!

WEDNESDAY WEDNESDAY WEDNESDAY

Brown Night

with Alan Brown.

Brown food, brown drink, and all the best in brown music.

Live set from Joe Brown.

Relive your brown memories.

£2 entry
£1 wearing brown

THURSDAY THURSDAY THURSDAY

Ladies night

Men Only - featuring the Mrs Full Monty Strippers*

50p entry (free bar)
*Prosthetic body sausages and man fur

THE MRS FULL MONTY
DIRECT FROM THEIR SELL-OUT RUN AT CLUB FOXXXY

FRIDAY FRIDAY FRIDAY

Line Dancing and Indoor Bar-B-Q with Chet Rescue and the Rancheroos

Can you tell what it is yet, pardner?

Country & Western, Bluegrass, Rolf Harris tribute act.
All the hits.
Featuring Terry on pedal lap Stylophone wobble banjo and didgerijews harp.
£2 entry

SATURDAY SATURDAY SATURDAY

Comedy Night

Compere: Bob "The Bowtie" Scampi - "The man with the memorable tie"

Featuring adult ventriloquist Bobby Slaggs - "The Discloser" "He'll turn your teeth blue"

with Bobby's friends:

Nipples the Llama
Cheapo the Swearing Sock
"Put a ****ing sock in it!"
Little Sir Eddie George The Ant
(uncensored economic forecasts from the Chairman of the Bank Of Ant England)

£3 entry

"Put a ★★★★ing sock in it!"

Too blue for TV, so he's not on TV!

Dungeon Working Men's Club, 4 Gash Alley, Dungeon, FR1 2BO
Tel: 01999 176822 and ask for Tony

The Framley Examiner

Framley's Traditional Favourite Sinc e 1978

ALL THE NEWS - ALL THE INFOMATION

"I FEEL INVINCIBLE" BELLOWS MAYOR AS JET-PACK EXPLODES

Freedom at last for Pam Ayres impersonator

By KATY BLIRDSNEST

FAMILY AND FRIENDS of

his political views had seen dark forces gather to hush the outspoken New Faces Winner impersonator, and abduction in M as little

Lonely old man under the hammer

By BUNCO BOOTH

A LONELY OLD man from Codge

ing in his pensive

off w.....
what he was told. One of the men two

is hoped will reach at least his reserve price. Overseas bids have been brisk

sidn't do

New police clampdown makes crime impossible

NEW MOVES by Framley police

in the direction of Madagascar

and made off

Ch Const Stanley Rosenda 42

NOW MASSIVE ECCLES CAKE BLOCKS M-WAY

M.O.D put on alert

by Adam Wrent

THE TROUBLED TALE of the new FR403 relief road opened a

another problem for the already grief-stricken stretch of road.

Only two weeks ago, magma from the earth's core began to bubble up through roadworks between junctions 27 and 28, and the southbound stretch was closed due to a swarm of African killer bees. Now there is the cake.

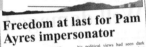

New move will "free up millions of pounds" says Mayor

Council opts out of local spending

by Jesus Chigley

proposals have met with resistance from nurses and teachers in the area but seem

Dog bites child's body off

"Toddler will recover" say liars

by Taunton Mishap

FRESH CALLS WERE BEING made yesterday for all animals to be

leaving only the head and a few inches of candy-striped jumpsuit.

However, a spokesman for the Sockford Association of Liars and Deluded People remained confident that the maimed tot would make a

FRAMLEY CATHEDRAL FOUND NAILED TO CROSS

by Challenger Putney

CONGREGATIONGOERS were

possibly the work of enormously strong vandals. Police are baffled as to how an engineering operation which detectives describe as "noisy" could have been carried out under cover of darkness without

Date	Name & Address	Comments
14TH July 1967	MR + MRS R. CLAWHANDLE, WHOFF	NICE
30 VII '67	Brian Maps, Next Door	Very Nice
15/8/67	KONALD STRENGTH	VERY NICE!
3-9-67	BONAPARTE FAMILY, CHUTNEY	QUITE NIC
12/4/75	Colin "The Cricketer" Smith	Nice museum
13 Feb 79	Steve & Jenny Hallo, St Eyots	Nice
27th July 8	Gavin Gavinessence	It's nice
3° Sep 84	Julia Something, Framley	I thought it was Nice
17TH Jan 1989	Paul Conference	nice & quiet
1 Apr 95	Actually Williams (née Mrs Williams)	Nice
18TH MAY 95	Military Pickle, Framley	Quite nice!
19th May 95	Mike Huff Martin Mcmccmclxviii	Very nice
~~95~~	~~████████████████████~~	~~████~~
19th May 95	Mr. Lemon Bradbury	Very nice
19/5/95	Mrs Plendid, Eyots	Nice !!!
19 May 1995	Candice Bawtik Albians, Whiff	On the whole, really rather
19th May 1995	Puth M. Scafe	Nice!
19 MAY 95	Professor Gideon Limeys, Melford-St-Malden	extremely nice.
19-05-95	ADAM TCHEK, WRIPPLE.	NICE AND NEAT
19 May 95	Patrick Bossert, Geneva	Nice!
19.5.95	Emily Quink, Sockford.	Nice.

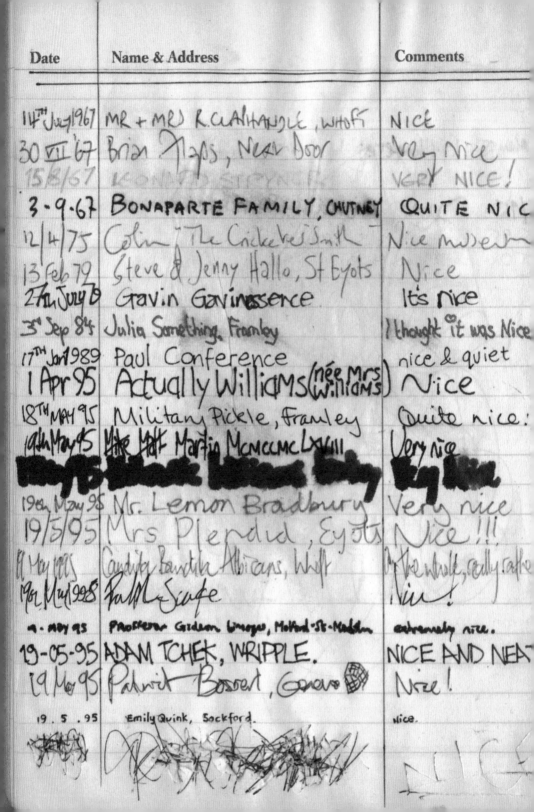

te	Name & Address	Comments
May 95	Holly Gollyollypop, Gubley	NICE
May 95	Evelknievel Williams, Crupfad	Quite nice.
May 95	Blaubery Bram, Franley	V. nice
/ 95	Joan & michael Joni mitchell wa	nice ! yes!
5. 95	Viscant Dr Le Compte 'fast' Eddie de la chevalier	C'est tres nice
5. 95	PUFFY BLAND WURLPLE	How VERY NICE
	Julian Robbin, Latford	Nice!
10	A pint of Cider Please	That's nice
11	ROWLAND WHITE PENGUIN ISLAND	I suppose its NICE
5. 95	Cat Ledger, WI IPE	100% nice
11	The CUNTS, Moford Govin	Nice!
11	Barbara Rubbish - Rubbish, Whipt	Awful yet nice.
	Daniel J. Don, Fromley	That's Nice
	Boxford Kit. Brownies	nice nice nice Nice Nice NICE NICE Nice NICE ice nice
v. 95	BUSTA HOODIE	nice FRY nice nice nice Nice Nice serve
.5.95	X	NICE
-5-95	THE PAYNE FAMILY - TELLY ADDICTS	AND THE YEAR? NICE
u	Arginator Straffard	Nice!
11	Martine Dry - Pasta	Nice !!!!1
5/95	Magnus Magnusson	H was nicest
11	Ben Piggret McDonald	Very NICE!
v. 28	Prof. Arthur Bostram ☺	Experiment Nice!

Notes

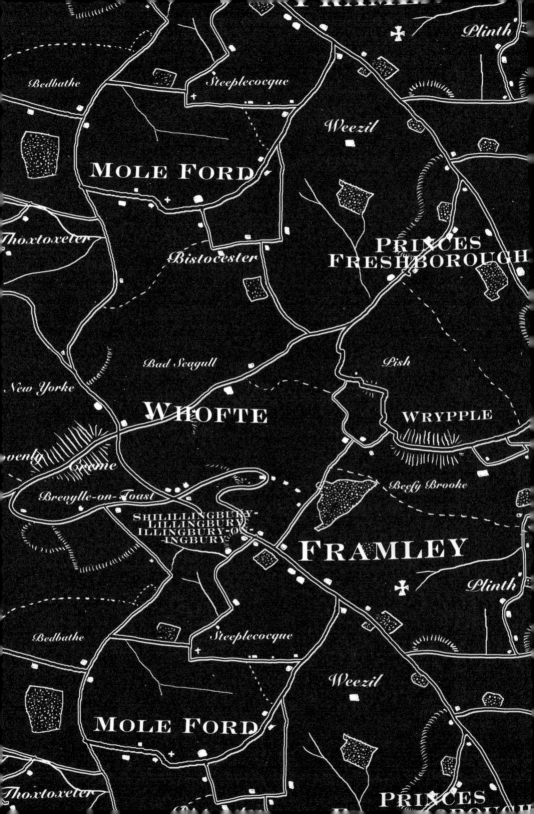